The  Book of
Outboard Motors

Other titles in the RYA series from Adlard Coles Nautical

The RYA Book of Navigation
Tim Bartlett
ISBN 0-7136-4409-5

This is *the* reference text for anyone following RYA navigation courses from Day Skipper through to Yachtmaster Offshore. By the end of the book readers should be fully conversant with what it takes to navigate a yacht or motorboat from one port to another safely and accurately.

The RYA Book of Navigation Exercises 2nd edition
Alison Noice and James Stevens
ISBN 0-7136-5255-1

A companion to the bestselling manual *The RYA Book of Navigation*, providing practice questions and answers at both Day Skipper and Coastal Skipper/Yachtmaster level. An invaluable back-up to anyone attending RYA shorebased courses and to those wishing to brush up their knowledge of navigation and seamanship.

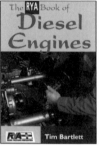

The RYA Book of Diesel Engines
Tim Bartlett
ISBN 0-7136-4847-3

Based on the RYA's one day diesel engine course, this book explains how a diesel engine works and how to look after it; for boat owners rather than experienced mechanics. A must for anyone who puts to sea with a diesel-powered boat

The RYA Book of EuroRegs for Inland Waterways
Marian Martin
ISBN 0-7136-5008-7

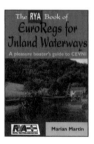

Written especially for pleasure craft, this book is essential for anyone travelling on the inland waterways of Europe. Covers signs, signals, flags, lights, buoyage, landmarks, procedures in tunnels, locks and weirs, and overtaking rules.

Other series titles in preparation

The RYA Book of Buying Your First Sailing Cruiser
Malcolm McKeag
0-7136-4205-X

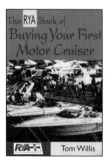

The RYA Book of Buying Your First Motor Cruiser
Robert Avis
ISBN 0-7136-5074-5

The RYA Book of Boat Handling under Power
John Goode and Dick Everitt
ISBN 0-7136-4894-5

The RYA Book of

Outboard Motors

Tim Bartlett

ADLARD COLES NAUTICAL
London

Published 1999 by Adlard Coles Nautical
an imprint of A & C Black (Publishers) Ltd
35 Bedford Row, London WC1R 4JH

Copyright © Tim Bartlett 1999

ISBN 0-7136-4848-1

A CIP catalogue record for this book is available
from the British Library.

Typeset in 10$^{1}/_2$pt on 12pt Concorde Regular by
Falcon Oast Graphic Art

Printed and bound in Great Britain by
The Cromwell Press, Trowbridge, Wiltshire.

Contents

Contents ....

Foreword

The tale with which Tim Bartlett explains the invention of the outboard motor is certainly more entertaining than the assumption that young Ole Evinrude was too idle to row across the lake or that he saw the massive commercial potential of his idea. The opening paragraphs of the book thus provide amusement, and the rest of the book provides a clear, concise and very readable guide to the modern outboard motor.

There are few things more pleasing to an owner than a sweetly running outboard motor. By the same token, nothing is more irritating than an outboard that won't start or is running badly, particularly as the chances are that the wind and tide will be taking you away from where you want to go.

Ensuring that your engine falls into the first category means, first and foremost, ensuring that it is properly maintained.

Regrettably, even then it can let you down and that's when you need to know how to fault-find and deal with the problem. This book will help you achieve the perfectly maintained outboard and provide the knowledge to solve problems when necessary.

In a clear, accessible style Tim Bartlett gives tips on regular DIY maintenance and what to do when things go wrong, along with explanations of best practice, some useful safety tips and the basic prinicples of two- and four-stroke combustion. One area where even experienced boat owners lack confidence is the choice of propeller; here the mystery is explained in terms that will enable even a complete novice to make the right choice.

I hope you enjoy this book as much as I have; you will certainly find it very useful.

Peter Dredge
RYA Motor Cruising Manager

1

...and all because the lady loves ice cream

There's a charming tale – though it's probably apocryphal – that says that the world's first outboard was invented because of a melting ice cream.

According to the story, a young American called Ole Evinrude was picnicking on the banks of a lake one warm summer's day in 1906, when he decided to treat his lady-friend to an ice cream. Unfortunately for him, but luckily for boat-owners ever since, the only ice-cream seller was on the far side of the lake. Young Ole rowed across with no problems, but couldn't row fast enough to get back before the ice cream melted.

Most young men would have put the whole thing down to experience and turned their attention to other things, but not so Ole Evinrude. In 1907 he produced a pro-totype outboard motor that could be attached to the transom of a rowing boat.

Ole's wasn't the first outboard, though: that honour arguably belongs to a contrap-tion invented almost half a century before by one of the pioneers of screw propellers, who devised a hand-powered 'outboard' that could be clamped onto any suitable boat as a means of testing and demonstrat-ing his propellers. Or maybe the laurels should go to a Frenchman, who demon-strated an electric outboard at the Paris Exhibition in 1881.

Evinrude's 'Detachable Motor', however, was the first to be produced in significant numbers, and that included all the main features of a modern outboard.

The main parts of an outboard

The main features of Evinrude's prototype motor have been copied by almost every production outboard ever since.

He used an internal combustion engine which he turned through 90°, so that its

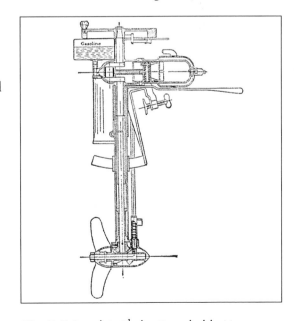

Fig 1 *Evinrude's 1$\frac{1}{2}$hp Detachable Motor as illustrated in* The Motor Boat and Marine Oil and Gas Engine *in 1912.*

output shaft pointed downwards instead of horizontally. At the bottom of the vertical shaft, he fitted a gearbox, from which a horizontal shaft emerged to drive a propeller. It was all mounted on a bracket that could be clamped to the back of a boat, but which left the complete ensemble free to swivel so as to provide a means of steering (Fig 1).

Sizes and types

Some of the most popular modern outboards produce about the same power as Ole's original – about 2hp (1.5kW). They provide the motive power for yachts' tenders and small dinghies and, as such, have to be light, cheap, and simple. At the same time, they also have to be reliable, and rugged enough to put up with the kind of abuse that few of us would expect any other kind of engine to withstand. Many spend most of their time languishing in the dark, dank recesses of cockpit lockers, or exposed to salt spray on the pushpits of cruising yachts. They are fed on dubious mixtures of fuel, oil, dirt, and water, and lie forgotten throughout the winter months, but are expected to leap into life at the first pull of the starter cord in the spring!

At the other extreme are the motors that are used to power high performance sports boats and offshore racers. These are very different creatures: they include some of the most sophisticated engines you are ever likely to come across, and are cared for and cosseted, tweaked and tuned to produce 200hp or more.

Between the extremes are a wide range of different sizes and types: outboards of up to about 10hp are often used to provide auxiliary power for small sailing boats, as a cheap alternative to inboard engines; outboards of 20–50hp are widely used on small motor cruisers and work boats, while engines of 40–200hp give lively performance on the sterns of sportsboats and ski boats.

With such a wide variety of outboard

The Tohatsu 9.8 is a typical modern two-stroke outboard, suitable for small RIBs, large tenders, or as auxiliary power for small cruising yachts.

motors available, it is easy to find exceptions to any sweeping generalisations. In general, though, outboards are best for applications where low weight and low capital cost are particularly important, and are least suitable for applications where running costs or the risk of theft are key factors.

Even these simple rules of thumb are changing, though, because they stem largely from the fact that most outboards have two-stroke engines (see Chapter 2). Increasingly, manufacturers are introducing four-stroke outboards, which are generally heavier and more expensive but cheaper to run. There are a few diesel-powered units that sacrifice almost all the traditional virtues of an outboard in favour of exceptional economy, and electric outboards intended mostly as low-speed 'trolling' motors for angling boats; at least one manufacturer produces an outboard with a small water jet unit instead of a propeller.

Why this book?

Modern outboards are inherently reliable. They are, after all, designed from the outset to cope with the marine environment – unlike their inboard cousins, which are almost invariably 'marinised' versions of car, truck, bus, or tractor engines.

They aren't infallible, though. Any engine will suffer if it is neglected: if it is left to rust; if its moving parts are allowed to jam up with salt, dirt, or cobwebs; or if the pipes and channels that carry fuel, air and water between its internal organs become clogged or start to leak.

It's trite but true to say that there are no garages at sea, so it's important for anyone who owns or operates an outboard to know how to look after it. If you can back up this basic knowledge of *what* to do with an understanding of *why* you are doing it and how the engine works, you're well on the way towards *not* becoming a Coastguard statistic.

The Basic Process: Suck, Squeeze, Bang, Blow

When you take the cover off an outboard motor, it looks complicated – and it is! But its complexity arises from the fact that when it is running, there are a lot of different things going on at the same time. Looked at in isolation, each of the processes involved is fairly simple.

One of the simplest and most fundamental processes going on in any internal combustion engine is the one that gives it its name. Fuel and air are burned in a confined space. As they burn, they turn into a mixture of gases and become very hot, so they try to expand.

The confined space in question is the

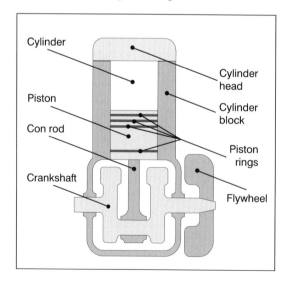

Fig 2 The basic structure of an engine.

Cylinder
Cylinder head
Cylinder block
Piston
Piston rings
Con rod
Flywheel
Crankshaft

cylinder: it's a cylindrical tube that is machined into a substantial metal casting, the **cylinder block**. One end of the cylinder is closed off by another casting, the **cylinder head**, while the other end is sealed by a sliding component, the **piston**. Springy metal rings, **piston rings**, fit into grooves around the piston, and press outwards against the walls of the cylinder to form an almost gas-tight seal.

The effect of all this is that the only way the mixture of hot gases can expand is by pressing downwards on the piston. The piston is attached to a connecting rod, or '**con rod**', whose other end is coupled to the **crankshaft**. Just as the cranks of a bicycle convert vertical movements of the rider's legs to a rotary movement of the wheels, the crankshaft converts the downward thrust of the piston into a rotary movement of the shaft.

One end of the crankshaft carries a heavy metal **flywheel**. Once the flywheel has started turning its momentum keeps it going, so the crankshaft keeps turning with it – pushing the piston back up the cylinder.

That much is common to almost all internal combustion engines. (There are a few oddball types, such as the Wankel rotary engine, but as they are not used for outboards they are outside the scope of this book.) There are important differences, though, between two-stroke and four-stroke petrol engines, and between petrol engines and diesels.

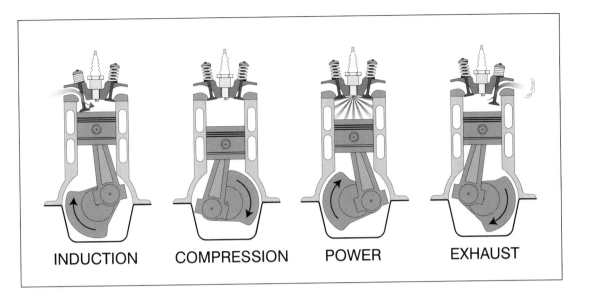

| INDUCTION | COMPRESSION | POWER | EXHAUST |

Fig 3 *The four-stroke cycle.*

Four-stroke petrol engines

Four-stroke engines are used in only a minority of outboard motors, but the proportion is growing every year. Although they are mechanically more complicated than their more popular two-stroke cousins, their basic operation is rather easier to understand.

In a four-stroke engine, the cylinder head incorporates tunnels which allow air and combustion gases to flow in and out of the cylinder. To stop the gases escaping when you don't want them to, the tunnels are sealed shut by strong, spring-loaded **valves**.

During the **combustion** stroke, in which the burning gases are expanding and driving the piston downwards, both valves are shut. Once the piston reaches the bottom of its travel, however, the momentum of the spinning flywheel keeps the crankshaft turning so it pushes the piston back up the cylinder again. At this stage, one of the valves in the cylinder head opens, allowing the burnt gases to escape.

When the piston reaches the top of its travel, the flywheel is still spinning, so the crankshaft now drags the piston back down again. The exhaust valve shuts, and the other valve – the inlet valve – opens. A mixture of air and fuel rush in through the open valve, to fill the ever-increasing space inside the cylinder.

The last stage of the process involves getting the piston back to the top of the cylinder, ready to start the sequence all over again. Both valves close, to stop the air-fuel mixture escaping, while the flywheel and crankshaft push the piston upwards, compressing the mixture inside the cylinder.

Just as the piston reaches the top of its travel, a spark of high-voltage electricity ignites the air-fuel mixture, so that they burn, expand, and drive the piston downwards to start the sequence all over again.

The four-stroke cycle, then, is made up of four distinct stages. You can remember them as suck, squeeze, bang, blow, but more conventional terminology refers to them as **induction**, **compression**, **combustion** (or power) and **exhaust**.

- During the induction stroke, the piston moves downwards while the inlet valve is open, drawing a mixture of fuel and air into the cylinder.

5

- During the compression stroke, the piston rises while both valves are shut, compressing the mixture inside the cylinder.

- During the combustion stroke, both valves remain shut while the air-fuel mixture burns, and forces the piston downwards. This is the only stroke that actually produces power – hence its alternative name.

- During the exhaust stroke, the piston moves upwards while the exhaust valve is open, allowing the burned remains of the air-fuel mixture to escape.

Valves

The work of the valves is vital to the whole sequence: they have to open and close at precisely the right moments, allowing an unrestricted flow of air-fuel mixture or exhaust gas when they're open, yet forming a perfectly gas-tight seal when they're shut.

Each valve is roughly mushroom-shaped, with a long straight stem and a flat circular head, whose edge is bevelled and precision-ground to match the slope of the hardened **valve seat** that surrounds the mouth of the

tunnel in the cylinder head. For most of each cycle, each valve remains shut, pulled firmly against its seat by a strong **valve spring**. It's opened, when necessary, by the **rocker**, a component like a miniature see-saw that pivots on another shaft running across the cylinder head.

Meanwhile, a component called the **camshaft** is being driven by the crankshaft, but at half the crankshaft's speed. On it are carefully-machined bulges, the **cams**, that are shaped and positioned so that each in turn pushes upwards against a rocker at the right moment in each cycle. As one end of a rocker is pushed upwards, the other end moves downwards to push the valve open.

Although the principle is standard, there are plenty of variations on the theme. The camshaft, for instance, may be driven by gears, or by a chain and sprocket system, or by a toothed rubber belt, and it may be positioned so that the cams push directly on the rockers; or further away from them, and relying on **push rods** to transmit the movement of the cams to the rockers. In this case, the ends of the push rods don't rest directly on the cams but sit in small bucket-shaped components, the **tappets** or **cam followers**.

Whichever of these applies to your particular engine, do bear in mind that the whole system will have been set up so that each valve opens and closes at precisely the right moment in the cycle. Small amounts of wear and tear can be corrected by means of a simple adjustment, but it's asking for trouble to tinker with the gears, belt or chain unless you know exactly what you're doing.

Two-stroke petrol engines

It seems rather wasteful, somehow, to have the piston going up and down like a yo-yo, but only producing power on one of its four strokes. The two-stroke cycle fits all four stages of the process into just two strokes of the piston – a single revolution of the crankshaft.

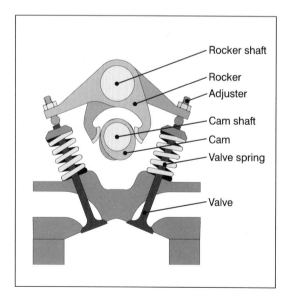

Fig 4 *Valve gear.*

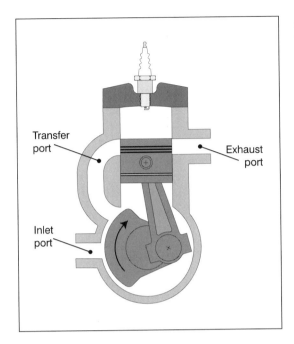

Fig 5 *The basic structure of a two-stroke engine.*

In a two-stroke engine, the tunnels that carry air-fuel mixture into the cylinder and allow exhaust gas to escape are not in the cylinder head, as they are in a four-stroke engine, but are cut into the cylinder block, with **ports**, opening through the walls of the cylinder. This means that there is no need for valves: the piston itself does the job of opening and closing the ports as it moves up and down inside the cylinder.

Another major structural difference between a two-stroke engine and a four-stroke is that the **crankcase**, which surrounds the crankshaft and the bottom of the con rod, has a particularly important part to play in the two-stroke cycle.

A two-stroke's crankcase is a sealed, almost gas-tight chamber, so as the piston rises, the pressure in the crankcase reduces, sucking in a mixture of air and fuel through a simple one-way flap – the **reed valve**.

Then, when the piston is dragged downwards by the spinning flywheel and crank-

shaft, the reed valve stops the air-fuel mixture from escaping. The pressure in the crankcase rises slightly as a result, until the piston uncovers the **transfer port** in the side of the cylinder.

The transfer port links the crankcase and the cylinder, so as soon as it is uncovered, the pressurised air-fuel mixture in the crankcase flows through it to fill the expanding space in the cylinder.

As the piston rises again, it eventually covers the transfer port, trapping the air-fuel mixture in the cylinder to begin the compression phase of the cycle. At the same time, of course, it's sucking more air-fuel mixture into the crankcase, ready for the next cycle.

The combustion phase follows, with a spark from the spark plug igniting the air-fuel mixture and driving the piston downwards, just as in the four-stroke.

In the two-stroke engine, however, as the moving piston nears the bottom of its travel, it uncovers another hole in the cylinder walls, called the **exhaust port**, allowing the burnt gas to escape. Very slightly further down its travel, the piston uncovers the transfer port, allowing a fresh charge of air and fuel to flood in from the crankcase, ready to start the process all over again.

There are four stages to the complete cycle:

- While the piston is in the upper half of the cylinder and moving upwards, it has covered the transfer and exhaust ports so fresh air and fuel are sucked into the crankcase while the mixture already in the cylinder is compressed.

- When a spark ignites the compressed mixture in the cylinder, the burning gas drives the piston downwards to produce power, while at the same time compressing the fresh air-fuel mixture in the crankcase.

- While the piston is in the bottom half of

the cylinder and moving downwards, it uncovers the exhaust port and transfer port, allowing the exhaust gas out of the cylinder and letting the pressurised air-fuel mixture in.

- When the piston is in the bottom half of the cylinder and moving upwards, it continues to drive the exhaust gas out, until it covers the transfer port and exhaust port again.

Pros and cons of two-strokes

The two-stroke cycle has a number of important advantages that are particularly relevant to outboard motors.

It has no need for valves or valve gear, so a two-stroke is relatively simple (and therefore cheap) to build, easy to maintain, light in weight, and compact. Its basic design is such that it can easily operate at almost any angle, so it is well-suited to outboard motors, in which the crankshaft has to be vertical, and the piston has to move horizontally instead of vertically. Inevitably, though, it also has its drawbacks.

One is that the highly-stressed bearings where the con-rods are connected to the crankshaft, and where the crankshaft itself is supported in the engine block, have to be well lubricated with a constant supply of oil. In a four-stroke engine, the oil can be stored in a reservoir or **sump**, pumped to the bearings, and then returned to the sump to be re-used. In a two-stroke engine, that is impractical because the crankcase is being used as a pump to handle the mixture of air and fuel, which would quickly flush the oil away. Instead, a two-stroke engine uses oil mixed with its fuel to lubricate the bearings, and then burns the oil along with the fuel.

The other drawback is that, although one would intuitively expect an engine that produces power on every revolution of the crankshaft to be more efficient than one which only produces power on one

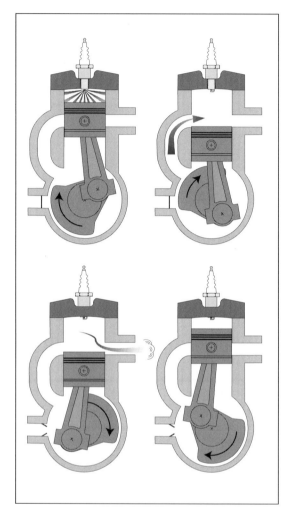

Fig 6 *The two-stroke cycle.*

revolution out of every two, that is not the case.

The four-stroke's laborious cycle and complicated valve arrangements combine to ensure that every cycle has a complete cylinderful of clean, fresh fuel and air. By comparison, a two-stroke rushes into refilling its cylinder before it has finished getting rid of the exhaust from the previous stroke. Some of the fresh fuel-air mixture escapes with the exhaust, and is wasted, while some of the exhaust gas stays behind.

Over all, the effect is that two-stroke engines use more fuel and oil than four-strokes of comparable power, and tend to be noisier. Not only does this make them more expensive to run, but it also poses a risk of pollution that makes them an easy target for environmental pressure-groups and the politicians that ride on their band wagon.

Scavenging

The key to both problems lies in the process known as scavenging, in which the outgoing exhaust gas is replaced by a fresh charge of fuel and air.

Engineers realised, long ago, that a two-stroke's efficiency could be improved by erecting a fence across the top of the piston to stop the incoming charge being blown straight out of the cylinder. This simple idea has since been refined into carefully contoured pistons and shaped cylinder heads, designed to guide the flow of fuel and air upwards from the transfer port, while sweeping the exhaust gas smoothly away. Engines like this are known as **cross flow** or **cross scavenged**.

An alternative design philosophy is known as **loop scavenging**. Loop scavenged engines have flat-topped pistons and rely on carefully-shaped transfer ports to swirl the air-fuel mixture around the cylinder instead of directing it straight towards the exhaust port. It is quite possible to design the ports so effectively that loop scavenged engines can combine high performance with good fuel economy.

There is a drawback, however, which is that because the speed at which the air flows through the transfer ports must vary depending on the speed of the engine, the pattern of the air flow inside the cylinder must also vary. This in turn means that the loop scavenging process can only be really effective at one particular speed – usually near the top of the engine's speed range. This characteristic makes loop scavenging

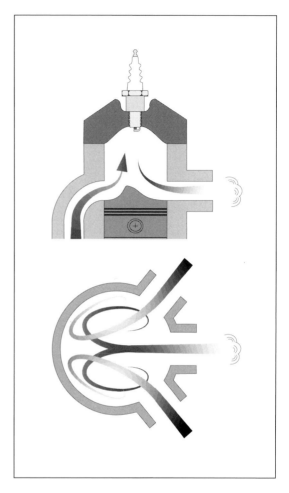

Fig 7 *Cross scavenging (top) and loop charging (below).*

most appropriate for very small outboards, which are likely to be used at full power almost all the time, and for the very large outboards used on high performance sports boats, where efficiency and fuel economy at full power are most significant.

Cross flow scavenging is more appropriate for engines which are likely to be used at a wide range of speeds, especially if they are likely to spend a lot of their time at much less than full power, so it is still common on the mid-sized engines used to provide auxiliary power for sailing craft, or for small motor cruisers and working boats.

Exhaust tuning

No matter how carefully the cylinder and piston are designed, there is no escaping the fact that the flow of gases in a two-stroke engine is very much less controlled than that in a four-stroke. In some very simple engines, without a reed valve, there are even some stages in the cycle at which the engine may actually be blowing fuel and air out, rather than sucking it in!

The reed valve provides some control over the air-fuel mixture flowing into the engine, but there's no obvious equivalent that can be used to control the exhaust, short of resorting to a complicated valve system like that of a four-stroke engine. There is, however, a non-mechanical alternative known as a **tuned exhaust**.

The principle behind this is that the regular puffs of gas leaving the cylinder set up pressure waves in the exhaust pipe, and that as each pressure wave travels along the exhaust pipe, there's a corresponding area of relatively low pressure following behind it. On an engine with a tuned exhaust, the shape and length of the exhaust pipe are designed so that at the engine's normal operating speed, the waves of high and low pressure act as invisible valves, with the low pressure wave sucking the exhaust gas out of the cylinder while the following high pressure wave stops the fresh air-fuel charge from following it.

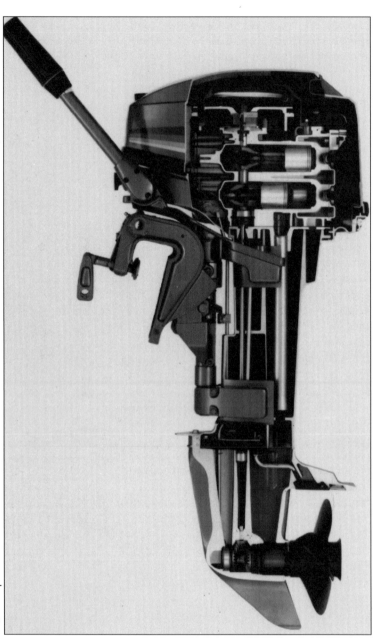

The vertical exhaust pipe running inside the outboard's drive leg is manufactured to a precise length so that the pulses of exhaust gas pressure within it act as automatic valves, to stop the incoming air and fuel escaping from the cylinder.

It's fairly obvious that this system will only work at one particular engine speed, so it tends to be associated with loop charging.

Diesel engines

In principle, and in structure, a diesel engine is very similar to a four-stroke petrol engine, but with one vital difference: a diesel engine does not use an electric spark to ignite the air-fuel mixture inside the cylinder. Instead, it relies on the principle that if you compress a gas it gets hot.

At the end of a diesel engine's compression stroke, the air inside its cylinder has been compressed to something in the order of 500 psi. Its temperature has risen, as a result, to about 800°C. At the critical moment, just before the piston reaches the top of its travel, the engine's fuel system injects a tiny squirt of atomised diesel fuel into this superheated air, where it ignites spontaneously.

Diesels are generally economical to run, and the fact that they run without relying on high voltage electricity makes them very reliable. On the other hand, they tend to be very much heavier than petrol engines, and the sophisticated fuel injection systems required make them much more expensive. The advantages and drawbacks of diesel don't really fit the requirements for an outboard motor, so although diesel outboards certainly have their uses and their devotees, they are still rare enough to be outside the scope of this book. (Try the companion volume *The RYA Book of Diesel Engines* instead.)

... Things to do

Safety
In general, when working on any kind of machinery you should be careful not to start it accidentally, and not to start it deliberately unless you know how to stop it. This is particularly true if you are working on an engine that has been partly dismantled, because you may have removed or disabled its usual controls and safety devices.

Wear suitable clothing – ideally a well-fitting boiler suit or overalls, and definitely no ties, scarves or jewellery that might get caught in moving machinery. Long hair should be tied back or tucked under a hat or headband.

If you have to run an outboard ashore, make certain that it has an adequate supply of cooling water, and that you and any spectators are aware of the fact that the propeller may spin like the blades of a food processor.

Never run a petrol outboard (two-stroke or four-stroke) in a confined space: the exhaust fumes are poisonous.

3

Fuel System

It is almost self-evident that if an engine is to run, it has to have fuel. Even so, the emergency services regularly find themselves rescuing boats that are drifting helplessly just because they have run out of fuel, while minor defects with the fuel system account for more breakdowns than any other single problem.

The system starts at the tank. From there, the fuel flows to the engine's fuel pump, possibly passing through a tap, a filter, and a hand-priming bulb on the way. The fuel pump's job is to make sure that a good supply of fuel reaches the carburettor, where it is mixed with the air that is being sucked in by the engine (see Fig 8).

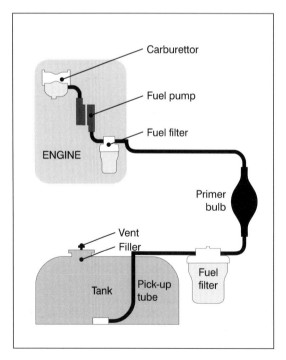

Fuel tanks

The fuel tank is probably the largest single component associated with the engine, but it is also the simplest – just a container in which fuel is stored until the engine needs it. Even so, you may come across any of three main types, each with slightly different features.

Integral tanks are permanently mounted on the engine, so their size is limited to about half a gallon or so. This, in turn, means that their use is confined to motors that are small enough to get a useful running time out of such a small quantity of fuel – up to about 5hp or so. Being mounted above the engine means that fuel can flow from the tank to the engine by gravity alone, so a tap is required to shut off the fuel supply to minimise the risk of leaks when the engine is not in use. The other important feature of an integral tank is that it must have a vent that can be opened to let air in as the fuel is used up, and closed to stop fuel being spilt while the engine is being moved or stored.

Portable tanks range in size from about three gallons to about ten gallons. The tank is connected to the engine by means of a flexible hose that can easily be disconnected so that the tank can be removed for refilling or storage. Like an integral tank, a

Fig 8 Schematic diagram of a typical outboard's fuel system.

portable tank needs a vent that can be sealed shut, but the fact that the tank and engine can easily be separated means that it does not need a tap: the clip-on connection incorporates a spring-loaded valve to stop fuel escaping when the hose is disconnected. On the other hand, it is very likely to be below the level of the engine when it is in use, so it needs a hand-priming bulb to fill the hose and to prime the fuel pump before the engine can be started.

Built-in tanks, built into the boat itself, can be of almost any size, so they are particularly useful for very large engines or for those which are likely to be in use for hours on end. One of their drawbacks is obvious: because they are permanently attached to the boat, they can't be removed for refuelling so you are committed either to buying your fuel from scarce and expensive waterside sources, trailing the whole boat to a garage or laboriously filling them from portable tanks. The other, more subtle snag is that it can be very difficult to drain off stale or dirty fuel and painful to contemplate the possibility that at times you may find yourself having to dispose of large quantities of contaminated petrol.

To cope with this eventuality, a built-in tank should have a drain tap, as well as a tap to isolate the fuel line. It certainly needs a primer bulb and a vent, though you don't need to bother about being able to seal the vent shut.

A couple of more subtle 'must haves' for built-in tanks include a fuel gauge to remind you how much fuel you have left in the tank, and a metal earthing strap joining the tank to its filler cap (or a special filler pipe that includes an electrical earthing strap). The earthing strap is an essential safety feature, because fuel rushing through a hose during refuelling can otherwise generate enough static electricity to produce sparks inside the filler pipe and tank.

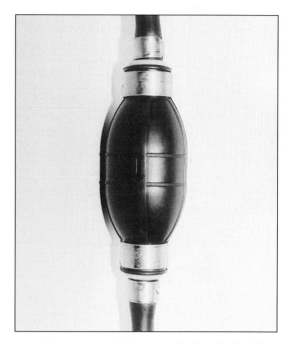

A rubber primer bulb is installed in the fuel line of any remote tank system: when squeezed, it acts as a pump to supply fuel to the engine before starting. Once the engine is running, its internal fuel pump takes over.

Primer bulb

The primer bulb is another simple but absolutely essential part of any outboard fuel system in which the tank is below the level of the engine.

Fitted in the fuel line between the tank and the engine, it consists of a flexible rubber bulb, oval in shape and with a non-return valve at each end. Repeatedly squeezing and releasing the bulb provides the engine with a supply of fuel on which it can get started and run until its own fuel pump can take over.

Filters

A typical two-stroke outboard of about 8hp may well run for an hour or more on one gallon of fuel, during which time each of

A fuel filter is a useful addition to any installation that uses a remote tank, as it reduces the risk of dirt or water getting into the engine's fuel system.

Most outboards have small in-line filters (the white bowl-shaped component just to the right of the pliers in the photo) to provide some protection against dirt and water. The component shown just to the right of the filter is a typical two-stroke's fuel pump.

its two cylinders may have burned 300,000 charges of air-fuel mixture. You don't need to be a mathematical genius to work out that the dose of fuel required by each cylinder for each stroke is just $1/600{,}000$ gallon. That's less than $1/500$ of a teaspoonful, or $1/25$ of a single drop! The carburettor has to control these tiny amounts very precisely, which involves directing the fuel through some very narrow channels and openings indeed.

It follows, from this, that some of the passages inside the carburettor can easily be clogged by tiny particles of dirt in the fuel, never mind the grains of sand or flakes of rust that so often seem to find their way into boats' petrol cans. To protect the carburettor against these, the fuel line is likely to include one or more filters.

Primary filter or strainer

Integral tanks usually have a strainer built into the tap assembly: it's just a slim tube of fine plastic or wire mesh that is intended to trap the coarsest debris before it leaves the tank. Portable tanks usually have a similar arrangement built into the end of the pick-up tube that extends down into the tank from the hose connection on top.

Built-in tanks don't usually have these devices, but may well have a separate filter in the fuel line, possibly with a water-trap as well. These filters can't usually be cleaned, but have replaceable cartridges or elements that should be replaced at regular intervals. It is difficult to be specific about how frequent those intervals should be, because different installations vary enormously, but in general terms you should be thinking about once a season or every 100 hours' running.

In-line filter

Many outboards nowadays include an in-line filter somewhere under the cowling. In a very small engine, especially one with an integral tank, the filter is most likely to be a disposable type that is intended to be unclipped from the fuel line and replaced completely when there are visible signs of dirt inside it. As a get-you-home measure, however, a clogged disposable filter can often be cleared by removing it from the fuel line and blowing through it in the opposite direction to the way the fuel is intended to flow.

A larger engine is more likely to have a slightly more sophisticated filter, with a fine gauze element that can be removed for cleaning by unscrewing the filter bowl that surrounds it from the filter head.

Fuel pump gauze

Some engines have a piece of fine nylon or metal gauze built into the inlet side of the fuel pump. This, however, is very much a last line of defence: if any dirt has got that far, there is something very wrong with the other filters that should be in the system!

Fuel pump

Not all outboards have a fuel pump: many of those with integral tanks rely purely on gravity to keep the carburettor supplied with fuel. You don't have to look very far up the scale of size and sophistication, though, before an engine-driven fuel pump becomes a standard feature.

The details of fuel pumps vary from manufacturer to manufacturer, and from model to model, but essentially they are all diaphragm pumps, which may be either mechanically or pneumatically operated.

Pneumatic pumps

Pneumatic pumps tend to be standard on two-stroke engines, because they are light, compact, and simple. Essentially, the pump

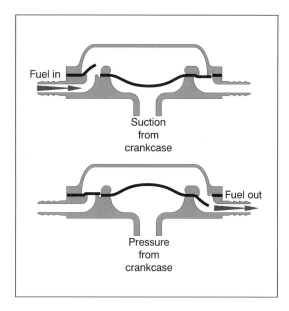

Fig 9 *The principle of a pneumatic fuel pump.*

consists of a metal body, divided into two chambers – one 'dry', the other 'wet' – by a flexible diaphragm.

The dry chamber on one side of the diaphragm is linked by a tube to the crankcase, so that as the engine's piston descends and the crankcase pressure rises, the diaphragm bulges outward (see Fig 9). When the piston rises, the pressure in the crankcase falls, and the diaphragm is sucked inward.

As the diaphragm flexes inward towards the dry chamber, fuel is sucked in from the tank to fill the increasing space in the wet chamber. Then, when the diaphragm bulges outward again, the fuel is forced out of the pump towards the carburettor. Small flap valves, usually part of the diaphragm itself, make sure that the fuel flows in the right direction.

Mechanical pumps

Four-stroke engines do not have sealed crankcases, so the pressure variations inside them are not enough to drive pneumatic pumps. Instead, they use mechanically-driven versions.

As with a pneumatic pump, the pumping action is achieved by a flexible diaphragm expanding and contracting the space occupied by the fuel in the wet chamber of the pump. The difference is that instead of relying on crankcase pressure to move the diaphragm, a mechanical pump uses a spring-loaded lever which is rocked backwards and forwards by a cam on the engine's crankshaft.

Carburettor

You could say that the carburettor is the heart of an engine. That would certainly convey the fact that it is one of the most important and complicated components. It would be more realistic, though, to say that the carburettors are the lungs of an engine – partly because most outboards have several carburettors (one for each cylinder), and partly because they are concerned as much with air as with fuel.

While the rest of the fuel system has to cope only with the relatively simple task of supplying clean liquid fuel to the carburettor, it is the carburettor's job to mix tiny quantities of fuel with relatively huge volumes of air in just the right proportions, and to regulate the flow of air-fuel mixture that reaches the engine.

As with most things on an engine,

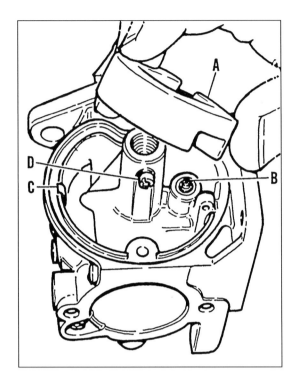

Fig 11 *Carburettor for 40hp Mercury outboard with cover removed. **A** float; **B** inlet needle; **C** baffle; **D** main jet. By courtesy of Clymer Publications, a division of Intertec Publishing.*

though, the principles on which a carburettor are based are simple.

A simple carburettor

An engine burns far more air than fuel. Even a little 4hp engine may well suck in some 15 cubic feet (over 400 litres) of air every minute – all of which passes through the throat of its carburettor.

On its way, this fast-flowing stream of air has to pass through a constriction, the **venturi**. In cross section, the sides of the venturi are shaped like an aerofoil, very similar to the top of an aircraft's wing or the lee side of a sail so – just like a wing or a sail – the effect of the venturi is to create an area of low pressure just where the flow is at its fastest (see Fig 10).

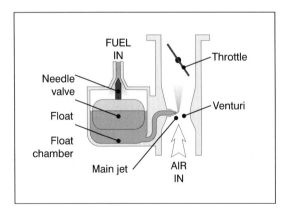

Fig 10 *The principle of a carburettor.*

Meanwhile, fuel flows into the carburettor's **float chamber** from the fuel pump. As the level rises, it lifts the float, which in turn lifts a tapered valve until, when the fuel reaches a set level, the flow is shut off completely.

A narrow passage called the **main jet** leads from the float chamber and into the venturi, so that when the pressure in the venturi falls, fuel is sucked from the float chamber to mix with the torrent of air that is rushing through the venturi.

Throttle and choke

To be practical, a real carburettor needs at least a couple of refinements, of which the first is some way of regulating the flow of air and fuel so that the engine can be slowed down. This is achieved by a circular flap mounted on a shaft that runs across the throat of the carburettor between the venturi and the engine. This is the **throttle**.

Unfortunately, when the throttle is closed to slow the engine down, the narrowest part of the carburettor's throat is no longer at the venturi, but around the throttle area: the flow through the venturi may be so much reduced that it either doesn't suck enough fuel through from the float chamber, or that it doesn't break the fuel down into the fine, even spray that is required for effective mixing.

Either way, the effect would be an engine that ran roughly or not at all at low speeds – were it not for another narrow passageway known as the **idle jet** carrying fuel from the float chamber to the area near the throttle valve.

The other important refinement is the **choke**. In some respects, the choke is very similar to the throttle: it too is a circular flap that can be opened to allow a free flow of air through the carburettor or closed to restrict the engine's air supply. The difference is that the choke is upstream of the venturi, so when the choke is closed and the engine tries to pull air through the carburettor, the pressure in the venturi area falls and draws fuel through from the float chamber.

So far as the engine is concerned, then, the effect of closing the choke is to restrict the air flow while increasing the proportion of fuel mixed with it – exactly what is required when starting the engine from cold. Opening the choke increases the amount of air, to weaken the air-fuel mixture for efficient running when the engine has warmed up.

Fuel injection

Increasing concern over environmental issues and the demand for higher and higher power to weight ratios has led manufacturers to introduce fuel injection systems to some of their biggest outboards. These do away with traditional carburettors, replacing them with electronically-controlled pumps that spray fuel and oil into the crankcase.

Unfortunately, whilst these EFI engines overcome some of the shortcomings associated with carburettors – such as the rather perverse fact that a carburetted engine has to increase speed before it can start drawing in more fuel – they still suffer some loss of efficiency by allowing unburned air-fuel mixture to escape through the exhaust port. Their performance tends to be better, but their overall efficiency is broadly comparable with that of a conventional two-stroke, and they are just as vulnerable to the impact of ever-tightening emission regulations.

At one stage, world-wide concern over engine emissions threatened the demise of two-strokes altogether, but that threat may have been averted by a new technology called Direct Fuel Injection, or DFI.

In principle, DFI involves using a high-pressure pump to squirt fuel straight into the combustion chambers. No fuel is injected until after the piston has covered the exhaust port, so there is no chance of unburned fuel being blown out of the exhaust, making the engine cleaner and more efficient.

In practice, two distinct variants of the DFI principle are being used. One, developed by

17

a company called Orbital, has been adopted by Mercury and Tohatsu. It uses a fuel metering pump, driven by the fluctuating crankcase pressure, to deliver fuel at about 90 psi to an injector mounted in the cylinder head. Meanwhile, another pump, mechanically-driven from the crankshaft, supplies air at slightly lower pressure to the same injector, where the air and fuel mix. At precisely the right moment, an electronic control unit triggers the injector, allowing a puff of very fine droplets of fuel and air to spray into the cylinder.

The other, developed by a company called Ficht, has been adopted by Evinrude and Suzuki. It differs from the Orbital DFI primarily in that it dispenses with the air compressor and injection pump. Instead, the injector itself acts as an electronically-controlled pump in which an electrically-operated piston drives a measured squirt of fuel straight into the combustion chamber at a pressure of up to 250 psi.

Unfortunately, although the principles of both are straightforward, the technology involved in putting principle into practice is very much more complicated, so fuel injection systems do not lend themselves to DIY maintenance or repairs.

. . . Things to do

Safety
Petrol is highly flammable, and gives off invisible but potentially explosive vapour. Do not smoke or use naked flames in the vicinity of petrol or in an enclosed space where petrol is present.

Prolonged or repeated contact with petrol or oil can cause a variety of skin disorders, including dermatitis and skin cancers. If possible, avoid it by wearing protective gloves or by applying barrier cream before starting work, and clean up afterwards using an industrial hand cleanser or household detergent.

Daily or pre-start checks
1 Check that there is sufficient fuel in the tank.

2 Check that the fuel hoses are free of kinks or damage, and that the connections between the engine and a portable or built-in tank are secure.

3 Make sure the vent is open on an integral or portable tank.

Periodic maintenance
Roughly once a season, or after every 100 hours' running:

1 Check all fuel hoses and the primer bulb for damage or deterioration.

2 Occasionally remove the end fittings from the hoses associated with remote tanks, and blow through the hoses with compressed air (or the pump for an inflatable dinghy) to remove trapped dirt.

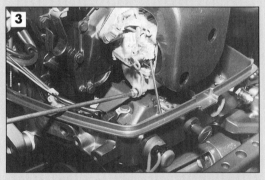

3 Drain the carburettor by unscrewing the drain plug at the bottom of the float bowl (if it has one), and use the hand-priming bulb or gravity feed from an integral tank to flush out any sludge that may have accumulated.

. . . Things to do

If it has no drain plug, you may have to remove the float bowl by undoing the screws that hold it onto the body of the carburettor. Be careful not to damage the sealing gasket in the process, and be careful not to lose the float or float needle.

4 At the start of the season, empty the tank and flush out any dirt or debris with a small quantity of clean petrol, before refilling the tank with fresh fuel.

5a On small engines with integral tanks, remove the fuel tap and rinse the associated gauze filter with a proprietary engine cleaner or clean petrol before refitting it.

5b On engines with disposable fuel filters, expand the hose clamps that hold the fuel hoses onto the filter by squeezing their protruding 'legs' together with pliers, and disconnect the filter. Fit a new filter, making sure that the arrow marked on the new filter corresponds with the direction of fuel flow.

5c On engines with 'bowl' filters, unscrew the bowl, remove the gauze element, and rinse with a proprietary engine cleaner or clean petrol before refitting it.

5d Some manufacturers recommend cleaning the fuel pump gauze. Details vary, but in general this involves unscrewing a central screw that holds a dome-shaped fuel inlet onto the top or side of the fuel pump, removing and cleaning the gauze filter, and then reassembling it.

Carburettor adjustments

Carburettors do not need frequent adjustment: it should only be attempted if there is a positive reason for doing so.

If you do decide to go ahead, refer to the manufacturer's handbook, and keep a careful note of what you have done so that you can get back to the position you started from if your efforts do not have the effect you intended. Where an adjustment involves tightening or loosening a screw, for instance, it is a good idea to count the number of turns required to tighten it (very gently) to its limit, and make a note of this before unscrewing it again to its original setting.

4

Ignition System

Once the fuel system has got the right mixture of air and fuel into the cylinder, and the piston has done its job of compressing it, all that is required to trigger the controlled explosion that creates the power is a spark. That is the job of the ignition system.

Unlike a car's ignition system, which uses a battery to supply the electrical power, a coil to convert the low battery voltage to the very high voltage required to produce a strong spark, and a distributor to direct the electricity to whichever cylinder requires it at any particular moment, the ignition systems of most outboard motors are based on a device known as a **magneto**.

Electrical basics

Electricity consists of a moving stream of minute invisible particles known as electrons, which can flow through metal objects (and some liquids, such as salt water) by jumping from one atom to another. They cannot normally flow through non-metallic substances such as air or plastic, so in order to achieve a continuous flow there has to be a continuous metal-to-metal pathway – a circuit – that the electrons can follow, and something to push them round it.

In a very simple electrical circuit, such as the one that operates a front door bell, the electrical 'push' may be provided by a battery, and the circuit is formed by the wires that link the battery, bell mechanism, and switch. The switch leaves an air gap in the **circuit**, so no electricity flows until someone closes the gap by pressing the switch.

In an engine, most of the circuits are less obvious; it may be reasonably easy to trace the wires that carry electricity to a component such as the spark plug or starter motor, but there is no obvious wire carrying the electricity back to complete the circuit. That is because the metal of the engine itself forms the return path. In electrical terms, it is often called 'earth' or 'ground', and on circuit diagrams it is often represented by a triangular symbol made up of short horizontal lines.

Volts, amps, ohms, and watts

Electricity flowing through a wire can be crudely compared to water flowing through a pipe. The rate at which the water is flowing is the **current**, and so is the rate at which electrons flow. The difference is that electrical current is measured in **amps** instead of gallons per hour.

The electrical equivalent to the pressure that drives water through a pipe is the **potential**: it is measured in **volts**, so you will often find it referred to as **voltage**.

A pipe imposes drag on the water flowing through it, and wires impose a corresponding 'drag' on the electrons flowing through them. Electrical 'drag' is called **resistance** and is measured in **ohms**.

The power required to move water around a closed circuit such as the central heating system of a house depends on the pressure that has to be applied to it to overcome the resistance imposed by the system and on the rate of flow required. You could also think of the power that you would get out of a turbine or waterwheel as being dependent on the pressure of water as well as on the rate of flow. The same is true of electricity: the power required to move electrons round a circuit and the power that they can provide once they are moving, both depend on the current and voltage together. It is measured in watts: amps x volts = watts.

Magnetos

A magneto depends on the very close relationship between magnetism and electricity.

Most people probably remember from school science that if you wind a piece of wire around an iron core (such as a large nail) and then pass an electric current through the wire, the core becomes a magnet.

The opposite is also true: if you move a wire through a magnetic field, electricity will be generated in the wire. How much electricity depends on all sorts of factors, including the strength of the magnetic field, the amount of wire exposed to it, and the speed at which it is moved.

A simple magneto, such as you might find hidden under the flywheel of an old single-cylinder outboard, uses exactly that principle.

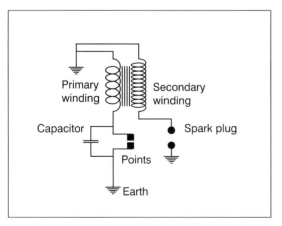

Fig 12 *A simple magneto ignition system.*

Powerful magnets are bolted to the inside of the rim of the flywheel, while the magneto's backplate, fixed to the cylinder block and crankcase, carries a stack of thin metal plates called the **armature**. Mounted on the armature is a cylindrical component known as the **coil**.

As its name suggests, the coil is made up of a mass of coiled wire, but it is really two components in one. The first, made up of relatively few turns of fairly thick wire, is known as the **primary** or **low tension (LT) windings**: the second, made up of hundreds of turns of very thin wire, is known as the **secondary**, or **high tension (HT) windings**.

As the flywheel magnets move past the ends of the stationary armature, they set up a constantly changing magnetic field around and within it. This, in turn, creates a flow of electricity in the LT winding.

For most of the time, the electricity in the LT windings is free to flow around a very simple circuit without apparently doing very much. The fact that it is flowing at all, however, means that it sets up a magnetic field of its own.

Included in the LT circuit is a simple mechanical switch, known as the **points**. The points are normally held closed by a spring, so electricity can flow through them, but at the moment a spark is required to ignite the air-fuel mixture in the cylinder, they are forced open by a cam (bulge) on the crankshaft.

Opening the points switches off the flow of electricity in the LT circuit, so the magnetic field it has created instantly collapses. To the secondary windings, the effect of this is just the same as a very fast-moving magnet: it induces a surge of electricity. The current produced is tiny, but the voltage is huge – several thousand volts.

In effect, then, the flywheel magnets and LT circuit are used to create electricity, while the points and HT windings transform the low voltage electricity in the LT circuit into a precisely-timed surge of very high voltage electricity, which is carried through a thickly insulated **HT lead** to the **spark plug**.

There are several variations on this theme, particularly in multi-cylinder engines, where the layout of the coils may be different, and the primary and secondary windings may be physically separated.

Even the simplest of practical magnetos, however, has one almost essential refinement known as a **capacitor** or **condenser**. In effect, it is an electrical shock absorber, to stop tiny sparks arcing across the points just as they start to open.

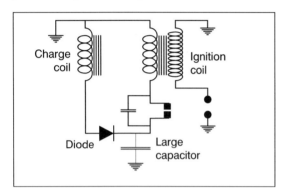

Fig 13 *A capacitor discharge ignition system.*

Capacitor discharge ignition

Capacitor discharge ignition uses the same principle of electromagnetic induction, but applies it in a different way. The electricity created by the effect of the flywheel magnets on the primary coil is used to charge a large capacitor.

If you think of a capacitor as a kind of electronic battery, and look at Fig 13, you'll see that as soon as the points close, any electricity stored in the capacitor will flow through the points and through the LT windings of the secondary coil.

This sudden surge of electricity through the LT windings instantly creates a magnetic field, which induces a much higher voltage surge in the HT windings that supply the spark plug.

In practical terms, the main difference between CD ignition and a traditional magneto is that in the traditional type, the spark is created at the moment the points open: in a CD system, it is created when they close.

Transistorised CD ignition

Traditional magnetos and CD ignition systems are simple and effective, but their points need regular and rather fiddly maintenance if they are to be reliable, especially in the damp environment that surrounds boats.

Solid-state transistorised ignition systems solve the problem. They are based on the capacitor discharge principle, but use an electronic component, a **rectifier**, to smooth the fluctuating flow of electricity from the primary coil, so that the capacitor is charged up much more effectively.

Their biggest advantage, however, is that the points are replaced by a transistor. In effect, a transistor is an electronic switch: when electricity flows to one of its three terminals, it 'switches on' and allows electricity to flow between the other two.

The electricity required to switch on the

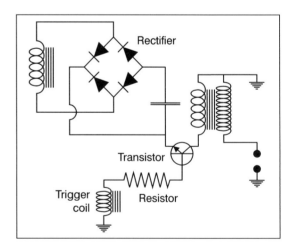

Fig 14 *A transistorised (solid-state) capacitor discharge ignition system.*

transistor is produced by a **trigger coil**, mounted on the magneto back plate so that it produces a brief pulse of electricity when one of the flywheel magnets passes it.

The effect transistorised ignition systems have had on outboard motors is dramatic. They have no mechanical parts to break, wear out or rust, so they require virtually no maintenance and are inherently more reliable. At the same time, the voltage that they can supply to the spark plug has increased to around 40,000 volts – roughly four times as great as achieved by traditional magnetos, giving a much stronger and hotter spark.

Perhaps best of all, they can be completely sealed, making them immune from the effects of damp, spray, or even complete immersion.

Timing

One might, intuitively, believe that the 'right' time for the spark occurs when the piston reaches the top of its stroke (called 'top dead centre' or 'TDC') and is about to start travelling downwards. That, however, ignores the fact that combustion does not take place instantaneously: it takes time for the flame, triggered by the spark, to spread through the cylinder. To account for this delay, the spark needs to be produced just before TDC.

Exactly how much time before varies from engine to engine and varies depending on the speed at which it is operating. At high speed, the spark needs to occur earlier in the cycle, to allow for the fact that the piston is moving faster. Typically, however, an outboard's ignition system is set up to produce a spark at about 5° BTDC (ie 5° Before TDC) at tick over, and about 30° BTDC when it is running flat out.

To achieve this change of timing, the magneto base plate is usually made moveable, and is mechanically linked to the movement of the throttle valve.

Spark plugs

The whole purpose of all this electrical and magnetic activity in the magneto is to provide a short pulse of very high voltage electricity to the spark plug – the component responsible for the all-important job of setting fire to the mixture of air and fuel in the cylinder.

Essentially, a spark plug provides a gap in the HT circuit; for electricity to flow in the circuit, it has to jump across that gap as a spark. The gap in question is between the spark plug's **central electrode** (connected to the magneto by the HT lead) and the spark plug's **outer electrode** (from which the electricity flows back to the magneto through the cylinder head and block).

In practice, there is a wide variety of spark plugs, few of which can be interchanged with one another. Five key features distinguish one conventional plug from another:

- **Thread size** refers to the diameter of the hole in the cylinder head into which the spark plug is screwed. The most common sizes (even on American engines) are 18mm, 14mm, and 10mm.

- **Reach** refers to the length of the screw thread – and even though the thread sizes are invariably in metric units, the reach is almost invariably measured in imperial dimensions such as $^3/_8$in, $^1/_2$in, or $^3/_4$in! If you use a plug whose reach is too long for the engine, it will protrude too far into the cylinder, posing a very real risk of serious damage being caused by the piston hitting the end of the plug. A plug that is too short is less critical, but it's unlikely to work very well, because the spark will be in the wrong place.

- **Seat** describes the way the spark plug forms a seal against the cylinder head. In most cases, a special metal washer supplied with the spark plug is used to form a good seal, but engine manufacturers are increasingly turning to plugs with tapered seats, that fit into matching tapers in the cylinder head.

The above three characteristics can easily be checked just by looking at the plug, but there are two more subtle features that can make a significant difference to the engine's performance:

- **Resistor** plugs incorporate a resistor that is intended to reduce electrical interference. They are becoming much more widely used, but may not work satisfactorily with old 'points' type ignition systems. There is no outward sign of the resistor, so the only way you can tell whether you are dealing with a resistor plug or not is by checking the manufacturer's specification.

- **Heat range** refers to the spark plug's ability to dissipate heat. Ideally, most plugs operate at a temperature of about 800°C, but the temperature inside the cylinder may be considerably more than this, so the plug has to be able to lose heat by passing it out to the cylinder head to stop the electrodes melting away. On the other hand, if it loses heat too quickly, the plug will be too cool, so it will be more likely to become fouled by oil, ash or contaminated fuel.

Air cooled engines, such as those used in lawnmowers and motorbikes, tend to operate at high temperatures, so they need plugs that can lose heat quickly: they are described as 'cool' plugs. Most outboards operate at much lower temperatures, so they need relatively 'hot' plugs, while engines which are used for long periods at low speeds, such as those on club safety boats or sea school training boats, may need plugs which are hotter still.

Surface gap spark plugs

One of the great virtues of the very high voltages available from solid state ignition

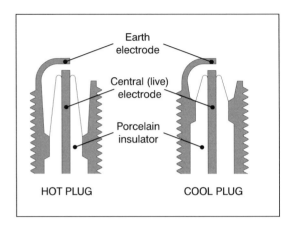

Fig 15 *In a 'hot' plug, the area of contact between the porcelain insulator and the outer metal body is small, so it retains heat. The larger contact area in a 'cool' plug allows heat to be dissipated to the cylinder head.*

systems is that the spark they produce is capable of jumping across a very much bigger gap than that between the electrodes of a conventional spark plug. This has opened the way to a new kind of spark plug, called **surface gap plugs**, which don't have an outer electrode at all: the spark jumps direct from the central electrode to the outer body of the plug. With a far bigger gap than traditional plugs, and no nooks or crannies in which oil or soot can linger, surface gap plugs have proved to be much more reliable than their predecessors.

Choosing spark plugs

There are only two ways to be sure of getting the right spark plug for your engine: they are either to replace a plug which has worked well in the past with another one of the same specification, or to follow the engine manufacturer's recommendations. These usually specify a plug suitable for normal use, and offer a suitable alternative for prolonged low-speed use.

The most common problem arises from the fact that although most spark plug manufacturers probably produce a plug to suit

A surface gap spark plug (top) doesn't have an outer electrode as such: the spark has to jump straight from the centre electrode to the outer body. This means it needs a higher voltage to operate, but is much less prone to oiling up than a conventional plug (bottom).

your particular engine, the reference numbers they use to describe it are likely to be different. A Champion L86, for instance, is equivalent to NGK's B6HS or AC's 44F. Fortunately, they all recognise the problem, and supply their stockists with cross-referencing books to 'convert' other manufacturer's codes to their own.

Kill switches

Every year, people are killed and badly injured by falling overboard and coming into contact with the spinning propeller of an engine. To minimise the risk all outboards (but especially those likely to be used on very small or very lively craft) should be fitted with a device commonly known as a **'kill switch'**.

It consists of a spring loaded switch that diverts the flow of electricity in the LT circuit straight into the metal structure of the engine. Closing the kill switch effectively by-passes the points or transistor so that there is no spark at the spark plug, and the engine stops. For the engine to run, the kill switch has to be held open, against its spring pressure, by a clip or key. The clip is intended to be tied to the helmsman's leg, wrist, or lifejacket, so that if (s)he falls overboard, (s)he takes the clip with him/her, allowing the kill switch to close so that the engine stops.

Stop switches

Taking the clip out of the kill switch is a perfectly good way to stop an engine: it is not an 'emergency only' procedure, and it does no harm to the engine. Many engines, however, have a separate stop switch for routine use.

It works in exactly the same way, and may even be combined with the kill switch. The only difference is that the switch is held open by a spring, and you have to push against the spring pressure in order to close the switch and stop the engine.

The kill switch is an essential safety feature. The switch has to be held open, against its spring pressure, by a clip or key that is tied to the helmsman's leg, wrist, or lifejacket. If he or she falls overboard, the clip goes too so the switch closes and the engine stops.

. . . Things to do

Safety

The ignition system involves very high voltage electricity. The current involved is so small that the total power is unlikely to be enough to inflict serious injury. It can, however, produce a very unpleasant electric shock which may make you jump enough to injure yourself by falling, or cause very small but deep burns. Be careful not to touch any part of the HT circuit when the engine is turning (no matter how slowly), especially if your hands are wet or you are in electrical contact with any other part of the engine.

Changing spark plugs

1 Pull the rubber or plastic plug cap (to which the HT lead is attached) straight off the plug, or, on very old engines where the HT lead is attached by a screw or nut, unscrew the connection to disconnect the HT lead. On multi-cylinder engines, make sure you know which HT lead goes to which cylinder.

2 Clean the area around the spark plug to remove any loose dirt, and then use a proper plug spanner to unscrew the spark plug. If you must use some other spanner, be very careful not to damage the plug's porcelain insulation.

3 Replacing a plug is exactly the same process, reversed, except that you should be careful not to over-tighten the plug: screw it in by hand until it is finger tight, then use a plug spanner to tighten it a further $1/4$ turn.

Cleaning spark plugs

Spark plugs are not expensive, so there is no reason why you shouldn't replace them at reasonably frequent intervals (about once a season) or for not carrying spares. Cleaning them is hardly worth the bother, except as a short term, get-you-out-of-trouble measure.

If you must clean a spark plug, wipe off any oily deposits with a rag dampened with degreaser, methylated spirits, or petrol, and then use a wire brush (ideally a copper or brass brush) to remove solid deposits. Wipe it over again and allow it to dry before refitting it.

Gapping spark plugs

Any conventional spark plug, whether it is an old one that has been cleaned or a new one fresh from the box, should have the gap between its electrodes adjusted before it is installed.

Engine manufacturers' handbooks usually specify the appropriate gap, but as a general rule it should be no less than 0.025in and no more than 0.040in (0.63 – 1.00mm).

1 Measure the existing gap by sliding the blades of a feeler gauge between the central and side electrode until you find one (or several together) that just fit.

2 Ideally, use a spark plug gapping tool to bend the side electrode to adjust the gap. If necessary, use a small pair of pliers instead.

3 Repeat steps **1** and **2** until the right gap has been achieved.

Servicing points

Points are cheap, so they should be replaced rather than cleaned. If you have to clean them, as a stop-gap measure because replacements are not available, they should be removed and their contact surfaces cleaned with very fine abrasive paper or emery cloth, before rinsing with methylated spirits. Different engines vary quite considerably, so the following instructions are only a general guide.

1 Unscrew any cover plate or parts of the starter mechanism from the top of the flywheel, to reveal large holes providing access to the ignition system underneath. Do not remove the flywheel itself unless it is absolutely essential to do so, but turn it until the points are visible.

If you have to remove the flywheel, unscrew the central nut that holds it onto the crankshaft, and use a puller (available from some tool hire shops) to pull the flywheel off the shaft. As a last and almost desperate resort, you could try replacing the crankshaft nut until it is just flush with the end of the crankshaft, and then giving the end of the crankshaft a smart tap with a mallet, while a helper supports the engine by holding its flywheel.

2 Using a pair of tweezers or small needle-nose pliers, unplug the wires that connect the points to the condenser and the coil.

3 Carefully unscrew the screw holding the points to the back plate (if you drop it, it may end up sticking to the magnets on the inner surface of the flywheel, so use pliers or tweezers to keep hold of it as you unscrew the last few turns) and lift out the points assembly.

4 Put the new points back in place of the old, making sure that any studs which locate them on the back-plate are correctly located,

With the flywheel removed, the coil (top left), condenser (bottom left) and points (right) can be seen. The points are held in place by a screw which is loosened to allow the points to be replaced or adjusted.

screw them down just sufficiently to hold them in place, and reconnect the condenser and coil leads.

5 Rotate the flywheel very slowly while watching the points, which should open and close as the flywheel is moved. Stop when the points are open as wide as they will go.

6 Use a feeler gauge to measure the gap between the contact surfaces, and move the base of the points assembly until the gap corresponds with the manufacturer's recommended setting. In an emergency, try a gap of about 0.015–0.020in (0.40–0.50mm).

7 Tighten the retaining screw firmly, being careful not to upset the adjustment you have just made.

8 If you removed the flywheel, replace it, making sure that the key which holds it in place on the crankshaft is in place, and that the flywheel nut is screwed down firmly.

9 Reassemble any cover plates or starter components that you removed in stage **1**.

5

Cooling System

All engines generate huge quantities of heat. Even the most efficient produce barely half as much useful mechanical power as is theoretically available from the fuel they burn and many are very much less productive than that. Most of the 'lost' energy is in the form of heat.

In everyday terms, that means that a 40hp (30kW) outboard is likely to produce at least as much heat as 10 typical domestic electric fires or 15 electric kettles.

All that thermal energy has to be disposed of, otherwise it would just build up in the engine, raising its temperature until its moving parts expand so much that they seize solid or weld themselves together.

Fortunately for us, outboards operate in an environment where they are surrounded by a virtually unlimited supply of a very effective coolant: water.

The cylinder block is invariably much bigger than the cylinder inside, so as to leave room for large open spaces between the walls of the cylinder and the outer walls of the block. These spaces are filled by sea, lake, or river water that is pumped up from the bottom of the drive leg. The water absorbs heat from the cylinder, and is pushed out of the cylinder block by more water coming up from the pump.

On some very simple engines, it escapes straight back to the outside world through a hole in the casting, but more often, it sprays into the hollow rear section of the drive leg, where it helps cool and quieten the hot exhaust gas. Most engines, however, still have a small hole in the block, with a hose or pipe discharging either through the bottom of the tray that surrounds the engine itself or through a hole fairly high up on the drive leg. The point of this is to provide a visible **tell-tale** jet of water to reassure the helmsman that there is cooling water reaching the engine.

Components such as the piston and crankshaft don't have the advantage of being in direct contact with the cool water, so they get much hotter. Even so, they are kept down to a reasonable working temperature by being able to conduct heat away to the relatively cool block.

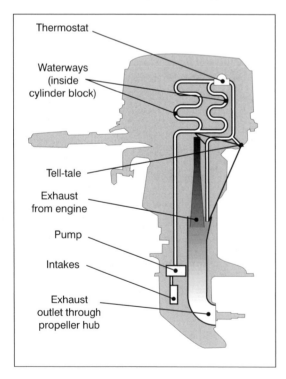

Thermostat

Waterways
(inside
cylinder block)

Tell-tale

Exhaust
from engine

Pump

Intakes

Exhaust
outlet through
propeller hub

Fig 16 *General layout of typical cooling system.*

The thermostat

One disadvantage of using water to cool an engine is that it can be too effective, especially when the engine is being started, or when it is running at low load. It is designed to run when all its components are at certain temperatures, so removing heat through the cooling system before they have warmed up would be counterproductive.

To overcome this, many outboards are fitted with an automatic valve, the **thermostat**, which regulates the flow of cooling water. It is usually mounted under a dome-shaped cover on the cylinder head. It's a simple component, whose only moving part is a circular trapdoor of thin metal, held shut by a spring. Under the trap door is a sealed capsule of wax or alcohol which expands as the temperature of the surrounding water rises until it overcomes the resistance of the spring and pushes the trapdoor open.

Thermostats can occasionally jam open or closed. If yours jams open, you are unlikely to notice the problem immediately: the engine will be producing less power and more smoke, and may oil its spark plugs more quickly than usual, but it will still run.

A more serious problem arises if the thermostat jams shut. Although some water will probably seep through, it won't be enough to cool the engine, which will overheat. You should spot that there is a problem because the stream of water from the cooling tell-tale will fade to a trickle, or start to turn to steam, but if you miss this the next sign may be a warning alarm – if you have one. After that, there may be no obvious symptoms until it starts to lose power or run roughly as it starts to damage its own cylinder walls, pistons, and bearings.

It's easy to test a thermostat by taking it out and putting it in a saucepan of water on the stove. As the water temperature rises, you should see the thermostat open. This

The thermostat is a simple heat-operated valve, located under a cover near the top of the cylinder head. Remove cover (top). Once the cover has been taken off (below) the thermostat can be removed for testing.

should happen when the water is too hot to bear putting your hand in it, but well before it reaches boiling point.

If the thermostat has failed, a get-you-home solution is to break the wax capsule and spring away to allow the trapdoor to stay open.

An outboard's water pump is located low down in the drive leg, so getting at it involves separating the lower unit from the drive leg itself.

The water pump

Almost all outboards use a flexible impeller type pump, mounted low in the drive leg, where it is driven by the main shaft that carries the power of the engine down to the gearbox.

The flexible impeller looks like a paddle-wheel, with several flat blades or vanes sticking out from a central hub, and is a tight fit inside its casing. The fit is made even tighter by a bulge in the wall of the casing, between the inlet and outlet ports.

As the impeller turns, each vane in turn

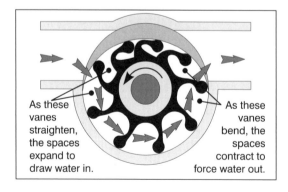

As these vanes straighten, the spaces expand to draw water in.

As these vanes bend, the spaces contract to force water out.

Fig 16a *The action of the impeller in a water pump.*

... Things to do

Safety
Work on the cooling system may involve running the engine out of the water.

For the sake of the engine, never do this without ensuring that it has an alternative source of cooling water; even a few seconds running without water will wreck the water pump impeller.

For the sake of yourself and spectators, be very careful of the exposed propeller. Do not put the engine in gear, and be aware of the fact that a big outboard's prop may 'idle' quite quickly enough to cause injury.

Flushing the cooling system
Ideally, the cooling system should be flushed every time the engine has been used, especially if it has been used in salt water. In any case, it should be flushed before the engine is stored for more than a week or so. There are three different methods, to suit different sizes and types of engine.

1 A flushing tank is by far the best bet for small outboards of up to about 10–15hp that can easily be removed from the boat. It consists of a suitable container, such as a metal dustbin or old water tank, filled with fresh water and fitted with a bracket to support an engine with its drive leg immersed to about its usual operating depth.

The outboard is simply mounted on the bracket, started, and allowed to run at a fast idle for a few minutes to allow the clean water to flush through its cooling system.

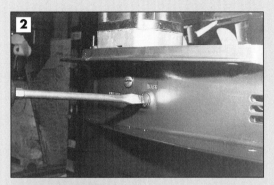

to a garden hose. The cups fit over the engine's water intakes, and are held in place by the springiness of the frame, so that water from the hose follows exactly the same route through the system as water from the sea, lake, or river. The engine can be run at a fast idle, but do check that the muffs do not slip off in the process.

2 Flushing adaptors are available as standard accessories for some engines. The adaptor screws into a threaded hole somewhere on the engine or drive leg and has a spigot to receive water from a garden hose. Check the instructions supplied with the engine or the adaptor to make sure you are screwing it into the right place, and to find out whether it is safe to run the engine. *If in doubt, don't.*

3 Flush muffs are widely available, and suit any engine whose water intakes are on the side of the gear housing. They look a little like ear defenders, or like a pair of big suction cups mounted on a tubular U-shaped frame, with a spigot that can be connected

Replacing the water pump impeller

So long as the engine is not started without cooling water, a water pump impeller should last many seasons. Nevertheless, some owners like to replace theirs as a preventative measure every season, while others wait for a reduced flow from the tell-tale as a sign that the impeller is starting to become worn. The exact procedure varies between different makes and models, but in general:

1 Disconnect the spark plug lead to eliminate the possibility of the engine being started by accident.

2 Unscrew the nuts or screws holding the gear case onto the drive leg, and pull the gear case away from the leg. The main drive shaft will slide out of the drive leg, and be left sticking up from the water pump housing in the middle of the gear case.

... Things to do

3 Unscrew the nuts or screws holding the water pump housing onto the gear case, and gently prise the housing free until it can be slid up the drive shaft.

4 Note which way the vanes of the old impeller are bent then slide it up the drive shaft.

5 Lubricate the new impeller (washing up liquid or a non-abrasive hand cleaner are ideal) and slide it back down the shaft.

6 Slide a new sealing gasket down the shaft, followed by the pump housing, and fit it over the impeller, making sure that the impeller blades are bent the same way as those on the old impeller before bolting it in place. (If in doubt, refer to Fig 16a to work it out.)

7 Carefully reassemble the gear case onto the lower leg, making sure that the drive shaft engages with the engine's crankshaft (inside the top of the leg) and that the gear selector shaft and water pump outlet engage with the shaft and pipe that hang down inside the leg.

8 Check that the gear shift operates correctly. (Turn the propeller by hand if necessary to help it engage while moving the shift lever.) Then reconnect the spark plug lead and test-run the engine either in a flushing tank or on the boat in water.

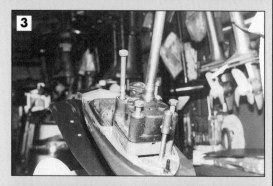

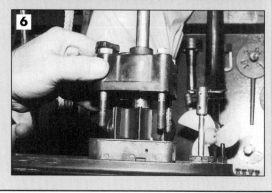

has to bend to get past the bulge. This reduces the space between the bent vane and the one in front. As the vane clears the bulge, it straightens out again, increasing the space between the two vanes and pulling water in from the inlet pipe.

As the impeller continues to rotate, the water trapped between the two vanes is carried around with it, until it reaches the outlet pipe. At this point, the leading vane encounters the bulge in the casing and has to bend again to get past it. This reduces the space between the two vanes, and forces the trapped water into the outlet pipe.

6

Lubrication

To the naked eye, many of the internal components of a new engine look highly polished. Seen under a very powerful microscope however, even the most polished of surfaces becomes a lunar landscape of jagged ridges and pinnacles called **asperites**.

They may only be as little as a millionth of an inch high, but as metal moves against metal the asperites on one surface collide and interlock with those on the other, creating the braking effect that we know as friction. They then bend or break to allow the movement to continue, creating heat that can, in extreme cases, send the surface temperatures soaring to over 1500°C.

Oil solves the problem by filling the tiny valleys between the asperites and separating the two metal surfaces with a thin layer of fluid. By doing so, it reduces wear, and allows the moving parts to slide over each other more freely. Then, as it flows away from the area, the oil carries with it any broken asperites, dirt, or chemical contamination from the fuel, while cooler oil flowing in to replace it absorbs at least some of the heat.

At one time, one of the major oil companies summed up this multi-function role of their product rather neatly in the advertising slogan 'cleans, cools and protects'.

Although the purpose and principle of lubrication is basically the same in all machines, there are quite fundamental differences between two-strokes and four-strokes in the way it is actually achieved.

Four-stroke lubrication

Four-strokes carry a supply of oil in a tank or **sump**. In the familiar case of a car engine, for instance, the sump is in the form of a relatively thin metal box, bolted to the bottom of the crankcase.

From there, a pump pushes the oil through a filter and then through a maze of oilways in the block and cylinder head to the various parts of the engine that need it. Once it has done its job, it drips back down through the engine to the sump, where any solid particles of dirt that it has accumulated can settle out as sludge, and the rush of air flowing under the car can cool it down ready to be re-circulated.

The oil system of a four-stroke outboard is basically similar, except that because it operates with its crankshaft vertical, but may be tilted to almost any angle, it isn't really practical to have the sump hanging down from the crankcase. Instead, the oil reservoir hangs down alongside the crankshaft, hidden inside the outboard's transmission leg.

Most of the lubrication system – like the pistons and main bearings that it serves – are deep inside the engine, and out of reach of a limited onboard tool kit. User maintenance is confined to making sure that the engine has a good supply of clean oil by topping up and changing the oil at regular intervals, and changing the filter.

In the longer term, it is a good idea to keep an eye on the oil pressure gauge if you have one, and certainly keep an eye and ear open for the oil pressure warning alarm. As

33

time goes by, some internal wear is inevitable, so the gaps between some of the moving parts will increase, making it easier for oil to seep away. This doesn't just mean that the lubrication around the affected part will be less effective: it also means that less oil will reach other components, leaving you with an escalating trail of damage throughout the engine.

Good operating practices delay the onset of wear: in particular it pays to remember that until the engine has been running for a few moments, it will be dependent on the oil which has been left clinging to its bearing surfaces. If the engine has been idle for very long, those surfaces may be almost completely dry, so if it is started with full 'throttle' and roars into life immediately, a lot of wear will take place before any new oil has had a chance to reach the parts it is supposed to protect.

Two-stroke lubrication

Most two-stroke engines can't use this system because they depend on having sealed crankcases in order to pump the air-fuel mixture into their cylinders. Instead, their oil is mixed with their fuel. It is pulled into the crankcase along with the air and fuel, where the fuel almost instantly evaporates to a vapour, leaving a fine mist of oil that lubricates the bearings of the con rod, crankshaft and crankcase. Then, it passes into the cylinder, where it lubricates the piston, piston rings, and cylinder walls before being burned and expelled from the engine through the exhaust.

This means that the owner of a two-stroke engine is likely to be very much

It's important to get the mixture of fuel and oil right, so some oil companies supply outboard oil in measuring bottles similar to those used for garden fertiliser and weedkiller: for small engines, it's a cleaner and simpler alternative to using a measuring jug.

more aware of his engine's demand for oil than his counterpart with a four-stroke; for him, supplying that need may well be the single most common maintenance job.

Pre-mixing oil
Most older or smaller outboards require the oil to be pre-mixed by adding it to the fuel in the tank, in ratios which vary from 10:1 (ten parts fuel to one of oil) to 100:1. Most reasonably modern outboards require a fuel:oil ratio of 50:1, but you should check this with the instruction manual: it is important because the addition of oil makes the fuel more viscous ('thicker'), so too much oil reduces the rate at which fuel can flow through the carburettor jets.

For engines which are likely to be used by a number of different people, it is worth marking the ratio on the engine (and on any cans or portable tanks), and setting out a very clear policy about whether fuel is to be stored mixed or unmixed.

The quantities of oil involved are quite small, so they need to be measured reasonably accurately: you can't hope to get it right by tipping oil into the tank straight from the bottle.

OMC Accumix (cut-away) fuel tank.

Automatic pre-mix systems

To save owners the chore of measuring and mixing oil and fuel by hand, manufacturers have devised various methods of doing the job automatically. The best known are probably the Autoblend and Accumix systems, in which the oil is stored in a reservoir fitted with a metering pump that mixes oil with the fuel flowing through it on its way to the engine.

Oil injection systems

More recently, manufacturers have developed more sophisticated ways of getting oil into the engine. In most of these, the oil is carried in a reservoir built onto the engine, with a pump – usually mechanically driven by a gear from the engine's crankshaft – forcing the oil into the fuel line. There are more variations on this theme than there are manufacturers: some inject the oil before the fuel reaches the fuel pump, others inject it into the fuel pump, or between the pump and the carburettor or even spray it into the air:fuel mixture between the carburettor and the crankcase.

Most waterside fuel stations (at least, those that sell petrol) have an oil dispenser whose pump is designed to deliver a measured quantity of oil with each stroke of its plunger. To use one of these, first check the quantity of fuel it is set up to mix – most give enough oil for half a gallon of fuel with each stroke of the plunger. Then select the fuel:oil ratio you need by turning a rotating collar on top of the oil tank. Press the plunger down a few times, to fill the hose with oil, before unplugging it from the top of the oil tank and putting it into your own fuel tank or can, and pressing the plunger down as many times as is required for the quantity of fuel involved.

If you don't have access to a dispenser, the traditional method of measuring oil mixtures is with a calibrated jug, but this tends to be a messy process, and leaves you with the problem of what to do with an oily jug when you've finished.

Probably the neatest method is to use the special dispensing bottle in which some brands of two-stroke oil are supplied (and some kinds of garden weed killers and pesticides!).

Although two-stroke oils are made to mix easily with fuel, it is worth putting the oil in the tank first, followed by the fuel. This is much easier than shaking the tank to ensure that it is thoroughly mixed.

Autoblend, Accumix, and the early oil injection systems that were in use until the early 1990s really achieved little more than saving owners the bother of mixing their fuel and oil by hand, but they paved the way for **variable ratio oil systems**. These really do represent a significant advance, because they allow the fuel:oil ratio to be automatically adjusted to suit the engine's needs.

At present (1999) most VRO systems use a straightforward mechanical linkage from the throttle valve to control the oil injection pump, varying the effective stroke of the pump to reduce the amount of oil it supplies at low speeds, but in future it is highly likely that this will be superseded by electronic controls.

Oil types and classes

It should be obvious from all this that although the oils used in two-strokes and four-strokes are doing fundamentally the same job, the ways in which they do it are so completely different that the oils for the two types of engine need very different properties. Four-stroke oils, for instance, have to withstand repeated recycling through the engine, so they need additives that will allow them to collect and absorb the acids that are produced as a by-product of burning fuel. For two-stroke oils, on the other hand, the main requirements are that they should mix easily with fuel, and burn cleanly.

Four-stroke oils

It is pretty obvious that if the oil is to do its job of separating two moving parts, there has to be a gap between them that the oil can fill. This, however, means that if the oil were perfectly fluid it would simply escape immediately through the gap, so to be effective, an oil needs a certain **viscosity**, or 'thickness'.

This seems to suggest that a 'thick', viscous oil is better than a 'thin' one, but that is certainly not the case: viscosity is an indication of the friction between the molecules of the oil itself, so a very viscous oil makes starting difficult, wastes power, and generates extra heat. In other words, you need to choose an oil of the right viscosity for your engine.

There are lots of different ways of measuring viscosity, but to make life relatively simple, oils are now graded according to a system devised by the American Society of Automotive Engineers (SAE), in which the higher the number, the thicker the oil. Your engine manual may specify, for instance, that it needs an oil grade 'SAE 40'.

The situation is made slightly more complicated by the fact that oils become less viscous as they warm up, so an oil that is the right viscosity at the engine's normal operating temperature may be very much too thick for easy starting in the depths of winter. To overcome this, it was once common practice to use a much 'lighter' oil in winter, and to accept increased wear as a penalty that had to be paid. SAE catered for this by introducing a second series of 'winter' grades, such as SAE 10W.

Oil technology has advanced enormously since the SAE grades were first introduced. Now, additives mixed with the oil make it much less susceptible to changes in temperature. This means that most modern engine oils can be used in summer and winter alike, and therefore have summer and winter SAE grades shown together, such as SAE 20W/50 or SAE 15W/40.

Even 'ordinary' engine oils nowadays contain a cocktail of other additives intended to enhance particular aspects of their performance. Inevitably this means that some oils are 'better' or 'worse' than others, so various bodies have introduced performance standards to identify oils that are suitable for particular jobs.

Of all these classification systems the one that is now most widespread (because it is the most easily understood!) is one that was developed by the American Petroleum Institute (API), which assesses an oil's performance in each of two categories: S, for spark ignition (petrol) engines; and C, for compression ignition (diesel) engines. As time has gone by, the capabilities of the oil producers and the demands of the engine manufacturers have increased, so now there are a range of API classifications from SA/CA (the lowest) up to SG/CE.

Most oils now meet SE/CC or SE/CD specifications, and are perfectly suitable for use in most engines, but if you are faced with an unfamiliar brand it's as well to check the quality designations printed on the can to make sure that it meets the requirements specified in your engine manual.

Two-stroke oils

For two-strokes, the choice is very much simpler: the main requirement is that it has to be an oil suitable for two-stroke engines. In most instances, this is very obvious from the name alone!

Nevertheless, there can be significant differences between the performance of one oil and another so – just as with four-stroke oils – various bodies have devised performance standards.

Once again, it was the API who started to make life simple for the customer, by laying down a simple scale of oil performance, ranging from TSC1 to TSC4. The 'TSC' stands for 'two-stroke cycle', and grades one to three covered different types of engine, ranging from small, low-performance engines such as those used in mopeds to the much higher performance engines used in racing motorcycles.

Grade 4 – the highest of all – covered oils intended for outboard motors. The reason outboards need a more sophisticated oil is that they are mostly water cooled, so they generally operate at lower temperatures than the engines on lawnmowers and motorbikes. This is good for the engine, but it makes it more difficult to burn off the oil in the cylinder.

The API grades were later renamed TA, TB, TC, and TD, before TD was taken over by the American Boating Industries Association (BIA) and renamed again, to become BIA TC-W.

Then, the BIA itself became the National Marine Manufacturers Association (NMMA), and later introduced two new and progressively higher performance standards: NMMA TC-WII and NMMA TC-W3.

The point of all this is that an oil suitable for a motorbike is not suitable for an outboard: it will do, as a stop-gap measure, at the risk of dirty spark plugs. For regular use you should look for an NMMA classified oil of the grade recommended by the engine manufacturer or higher. In any case,

at present (1999) you can't go wrong by using an oil labelled TC-W3.

Gear oils

The gearbox, located just in front of the propeller, needs lubrication too, but its operating conditions are different from those of the engine, so it needs a different kind of oil – usually one of much higher viscosity, and with additives intended to stop it being squeezed out from between metal surfaces when subjected to the very high loads that are involved in transmitting the power of the engine to the propeller.

For most outboards the right oil is one labelled SAE 90 Hypoid, but there are a few exceptions: some very high performance motors, for instance, require a much higher viscosity gear oil, as do some older models such as the British Seagull Featherweight and Century ranges.

Grease

Grease is not just 'thick' oil: it is oil to which some form of thickener, such as soap, has been added, along with a cocktail of other chemicals such as molybdenum disulphide or zinc oxide that are intended to enhance particular characteristics such as its ability to stick to metal surfaces, or to resist water, or to withstand high temperatures. Nor is it a substitute for oil: because it is very much thicker, it cannot be used in components that are moving at very high speeds, because it would generate too much heat by internal friction; eventually, the oil would burn off to leave only the thickener behind.

So far as outboards are concerned, however, grease is an important lubricant for various low-speed joints such as the clamps which hold the engine onto the boat, the tilt and swivel pins, and the control linkages. It also provides important protection against corrosion for exposed bare metal surfaces such as the propeller shaft.

37

None of these are particularly demanding applications, so almost any grease will do, especially if it is one that has additives to make it particularly suitable for marine use such as Duckham's Keenol or any of the 'own brand' greases distributed by outboard manufacturers.

There is one big exception to this: *Never, ever, use a graphite grease on any marine equipment.*

Graphite is added to many greases because it improves their lubricating properties: it's a naturally 'slippery' solid. Unfortunately, when it is in contact with metal and sea water, it sets up a chemical reaction which eats away the metal very quickly.

Applying grease

There are two ways to apply grease: by hand or by grease gun.

Hand application is appropriate when the surfaces to be greased are easily accessible, such as control linkages and the propeller shaft. The thing to avoid is overdoing it: a thin, even smear of grease is much more effective than a big dollop of it in one place. A small paintbrush is useful for this, especially as it saves covering yourself with grease as well as the engine!

For enclosed surfaces such as the tilt and swivel pins, there is no practical alternative to a grease gun, which forces grease into the area through a small, spring-loaded non-return valve called a grease nipple.

. . . Things to do

Safety

The additives that make modern oils better for your engine make them worse for you. Take care to avoid unnecessary or prolonged contact with oil – new or used.

Remember that petrol, and the vapour that comes from it, is highly flammable. Do not smoke when pouring or mixing fuel, avoid naked flames or sparks, and do not attempt to top up an integral fuel tank while the engine is running.

Checking oil level (four-strokes only)

Check the oil level each day the engine is to be used. It is quite normal for an engine to 'use' a certain amount of oil, but a sudden increase in the rate of consumption may indicate the onset of a serious problem which should be checked by a professional.

1 Withdraw the dipstick, wipe it with a dry rag and put it back, making sure it is pushed fully home. Pull it out again, and look at the oil level, which should be between the 'max' and 'min' marks. Then replace the dipstick.

2 If necessary, top up the oil by pouring oil in through the filler cap, which is usually pretty conspicuous, high up on one side of the engine. Leave the engine for a few seconds for the new oil to drain down before re-checking the level.

... Things to do

Changing the oil and filter (four-strokes only)

The oil and filter should be changed at the end of each season, or after about 100 hours' use.

1 First run the engine up to operating temperature, then protect the area around the filter from spillages. Try to avoid contact with the used oil.

2 Unscrew the filter, ideally using a strap or chain wrench. If that isn't available or doesn't work, drive a large screwdriver through the canister, just off centre, and use it as a lever.

3 Smear the sealing ring on the new filter with a thin film of fresh oil, and spin the filter on until the sealing ring just touches the filter head, before tightening it another half turn by hand. Do not over-tighten it.

4 Drain the oil, by placing a suitable container (such as an old ice-cream carton) under the drain plug (usually at the back of the motor's drive leg, just below the engine) and unscrewing the drain plug to allow the oil to run out into the container.

5 Shut the drain plug, and then top up with fresh oil of the type specified by the engine manufacturer. If in doubt, use a good quality oil of SAE 10W40 grade.

6 When you next run the engine, keep its speed down to tick-over for a few minutes, and then inspect for leaks around the filter. Even if no leaks appear, check the oil level and top it up, because some oil will be retained in the filter.

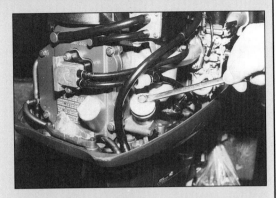
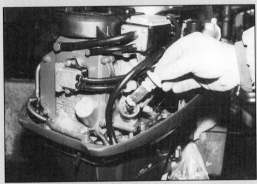
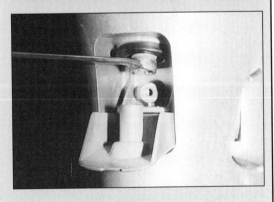

The photos (top and centre) show the changing of an element-type oil filter where only the element is replaced. The bottom photo shows the drain plug being unscrewed.

. . . Things to do

Looking after auto-mixing systems (two-strokes only)

Some automatic mixing systems are virtually 'maintenance free', but others are not. Unfortunately, there are so many significant but detailed differences that maintenance of the many different auto-mix systems is outside the scope of this book. Make sure you check with the manufacturer's handbook!

Checking and changing gearbox oil (all outboards)

Gearbox oil should be checked every 2–3 months if the motor is in regular use, and should be changed at the start of the winter.

1 Stand the engine upright – that is, in its normal running position – and remove upper 'vent' or 'level' plug (usually on the same side of the leg, but higher up, and roughly level with the anti-ventilation plate above the propeller). Note that some engines have two vent plugs.

2 Unscrew the drain plug, usually labelled, at the bottom of the leg below the gearbox and just above the skeg. Allow a drop or two of oil to escape, and inspect it:

- If the oil is 'milky' then it has been contaminated with water: the oil seal around the propeller shaft probably needs replacing.

- If it feels 'gritty' then the gearbox is probably being damaged by misuse. Drain the gear oil, refill, and find out why the damage is occurring.

3 To drain the oil, remove the drain plug.

4 Once the oil has drained, refill by pumping oil in through the drain hole. For do-it-yourselfers, outboard oil is available in tubes to make this a simple process, but a professional is more likely to use a purpose-made pump.

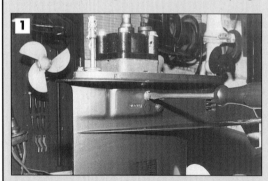

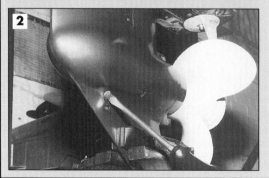

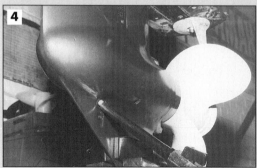

. . . Things to do

5 When the level is correct, excess oil will seep from the vent.

6 Replace the plug in the vent hole, followed by the drain plug. (If your engine has two vents, replace the plug in the first hole that oil appears from, and then carry on until oil appears at the second one.)

Greasing (all outboards)

There are many differences between individual makes and models, so you should consult the manufacturer's handbook if possible. In general, you should grease the following points about once per season:

1 Swivel and tilt pins.

2 Clamp screws.

3 Reverse lock (the linkage that hold the engine down when astern gear is engaged).

4 Steering cable and joints.

5 Throttle cable and joints (including the shaft and gears inside the tiller if it has a twist-grip throttle).

6 Exposed parts of the gear shift mechanism.

7 Remove the propeller and grease the shaft.

Bear in mind that if the old grease has been exposed to air or salt, it will have dried out and may be contaminated, so you will achieve very little by putting fresh grease on top: clean off the old grease first!

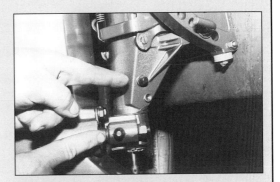

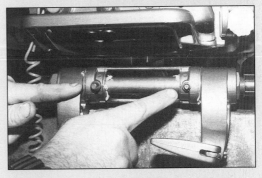

Grease is used to protect and lubricate exposed low-speed parts: on the engine shown above, two grease nipples serve the swivel bracket (top); two more serve the tilt bracket (bottom)... but check your manual.

7

Starters and Electrics

They are getting fewer and further between, but there are still a fair number of engines around whose flywheels are exposed, and which are started by pulling a cord that has to be wound around the flywheel by hand.

One step up in sophistication is a **recoil starter system**, used on most engines up to about 10hp, and on some of 50hp or more, in which the starter cord rewinds automatically. Above 50hp, electric start is pretty well standard, but most engines have some facility for reverting to the old-fashioned rope system for use in emergencies.

Recoil starters

The principle of a recoil starter is simple: the starter cord is wound around a pulley, mounted on the engine's flywheel. When the pulley is turned by pulling the cord, a

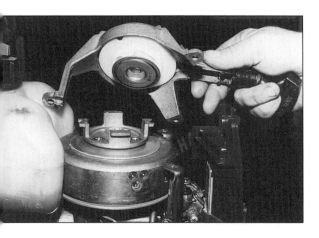

A recoil starter is a simple, rope-operated mechanism for starting small engines (up to about 40hp).

ratchet mechanism locks it onto the flywheel. Then, when the engine starts, or the cord is released, the ratchet disengages and a coil spring turns the pulley in the opposite direction to rewind the cord. On all but the very smallest and simplest engines, a safety lock is incorporated, to stop the starter from being turned when the engine is in gear.

The details, however, vary between different makes and models. In some, the ratchet mechanism and rewind springs are enclosed in a thin metal casing, and if anything goes wrong with it, the complete cartridge has to be replaced. In others, the various components are more exposed, so the whole assembly can be dismantled for repairs or maintenance.

Motors and generators

Electric starting, in which an electric motor provides the physical effort required to start the engine, has obvious advantages but there is a price to be paid, both in the increased price of an electric start engine, and in the increased complexity of the electrical system. Not only is there the starter motor itself, and its associated wiring: it has to have a battery, to provide the power, and some means of recharging the battery ready for the next start.

First principles
Like a magneto (Chapter 4), generators and starter motors depend on the very close relationship between magnetism and electricity, which can be summed up by saying that

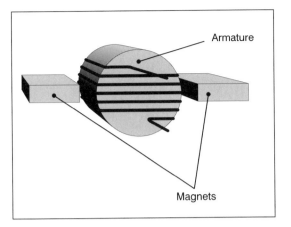

Fig 17 *The principle of a generator or motor.*

if you move a wire in a magnetic field you'll
create electricity, and if you pass electricity
through a wire you'll create magnetism.

Fig 17 shows how this might be applied
to make electricity: a coil of wire, wound
around a central core, is spinning in the
magnetic field between two magnets. As it
rotates, the wires that make up the coil
move through the magnetic field, to generate an electric current.

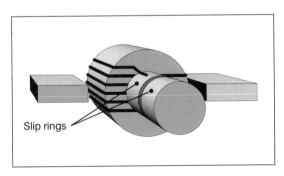

Fig 18 *A simple generator.*

Fig 18 shows one way of getting the electricity out of the coil: the ends of the wire
are connected to brass slip rings, fixed to
the spinning shaft. Self-lubricating carbon
brushes press against the slip rings to collect the electricity, and wires take it away to
the rest of the system.

*An outboard's alternator does not look at all
like that on a car, and is usually hidden by the
flywheel, whose magnets move quickly past the
ends of the alternator coil to create electricity.*

Alternators

In practice, outboard motors do not use the
kind of generator shown in Fig 18. Instead,
they use a device called an **alternator**, based
on the same principles, but with the whole
structure turned inside out: several coils
are fixed to the crankcase in a circular
arrangement known as a **stator**, while the
magnets – the same ones as used by the
magneto – are fixed to the inside of the flywheel.

One slight snag with this arrangement is
that the flow of electricity it produces is
constantly changing direction: in other
words it is AC (alternating current) rather
than DC (direct current). If the electricity is
only to be used to power lights while the
engine is running, that is no problem.
Unfortunately, batteries can only store DC
electricity, so a motor fitted with what manufacturers often call a 'lighting coil' cannot
be used to charge a battery.

To overcome this, most outboards' electrical system includes an extra component
called a **rectifier**, which acts as a kind of one-
way valve, turning the alternating flow of
current into a fluctuating but one-way flow.

The starter motor is mounted alongside the cylinder block: a gear on its shaft (hidden by a cover) engages with matching teeth on the engine's flywheel.

Starter motors

Structurally, an electric motor is very much more like the rudimentary generator in Fig 18: it has coils of wire mounted on a central shaft called the **armature**, and magnets mounted inside the casing to create a magnetic field. Instead of slip rings, however, it uses a segmented **commutator** to conduct electricity from the brushes to the coils.

The big difference is that a motor uses electricity instead of creating it! When a current is passed through the armature coils, it creates a magnetic field which interacts with the magnetic field set up by the field windings in such a way that the armature is forced to rotate.

The connection between the starter motor and the engine is achieved by an arrangement known as a **bendix**, made up of a cog (called a **pinion**) that can slide along a spiral groove machined into the motor's shaft. While the motor is stopped, a spring holds the pinion down towards the starter body by a spring. As the motor starts to turn, however, the pinion takes time to catch up, so for a fraction of a second it is turning more slowly than the shaft on which it is mounted. As a result, the spiral groove in the shaft screws its way through the pinion, forcing it away from the starter body to engage with a circle of matching teeth (called the *ring gear*) on the engine's flywheel. As soon as the engine starts, the ring gear drives the pinion faster than the motor is turning, so the opposite happens: the pinion screws its way back down the starter shaft to disengage itself from the ring gear.

Batteries

We can't create energy, we can only convert it from one form into another. That is what happens inside the engine itself: chemical energy is released from the burning fuel and converted into mechanical energy. The alternator then converts some of that mechanical energy into electrical energy. Electrical energy, however, can't be stored; to achieve that effect, the battery has to convert it back into chemical energy.

There are lots of ways of doing this, including the lightweight nickel-cadmium (NiCad) and nickel-metal hydride (NiMH) batteries used for mobile phones and hand-held radios. For the time being, however, these are too expensive to be used to store large amounts of power, so boats almost invariably use relatively cheap, low-tech **lead-acid** batteries.

The working part of a fully-charged lead-acid battery is a stack of lead plates, inter-leaved with layers of lead peroxide and porous separators and surrounded by sulphuric acid. The acid tries to convert both sets of plates into lead sulphate while converting itself into water by rearranging the electrical charges that hold the molecules together. In the process, it creates an electric current between the positive peroxide plates and the negative lead plates.

Eventually, the sulphuric acid becomes so dilute that the reaction stops. The battery is then described as 'flat'. The beauty of the lead-acid battery, however, is that the whole process can be reversed by using the alternator to push electricity through it in the opposite direction. This converts the lead sulphate back into lead and lead peroxide, while the left-over sulphate turns the water back into sulphuric acid.

The system isn't absolutely perfect, though. For one thing, the conversion process is never 100% completed; repeated charging and discharging leaves some unconverted lead sulphate on the plates, gradually reducing the battery's ability to 'hold its charge'. Eventually, the accumulated lead sulphate flakes away, to lie useless in the bottom of the casing.

Another problem is that passing electricity through water – or through a solution of sulphuric acid in water – causes a process known as electrolysis, which breaks down the water into hydrogen and oxygen. For safety reasons, this potentially explosive mixture of gases should be vented overboard, but it's important to appreciate that the venting effectively discharges water from the battery, which will have to be topped up with distilled or de-ionised water from time to time.

The demands of starting an engine are very different from those imposed by 'ship's services' such as lighting and navigation equipment; the starter motor demands a lot of current for a few seconds at a time, while domestic and navigation equipment draws a relatively tiny current for hours at a stretch. Ideally, these contrasting requirements call for two different types of battery: a **heavy duty** battery for engine starting, and a **deep cycle** battery for domestic loads.

Structurally, the two types differ mainly in the number and thickness of their plates: a heavy duty battery has a large number of relatively thin plates, in order to expose as much surface area to the acid as possible, while a deep cycle battery has a smaller number of thicker plates in order to withstand the long term effects of sulphation caused by being repeatedly discharged almost to the stage of being 'flat'. 'Marine' batteries are a halfway house, intended mainly for small boats on which one battery may have to do both jobs.

Electrical systems

Whenever an electric current passes through a wire it creates heat – and the heavier the current or the thinner the wire, the hotter it is likely to get. Taken to extremes, this could melt the insulation around the wire, or even start a fire. To stop this happening, a well-designed electrical system has cables that are big enough to allow heat to radiate away from the wire naturally.

Fuses and circuit breakers

There is still an element of risk, though, because the current could – for all sorts of reasons – increase to levels far greater than the designer envisaged. To make sure this does not happen, the system should incorporate either a **fuse** or a **circuit breaker**.

A fuse is a short piece of thin wire built into the system as a weak link that will heat up and break before the rest of the system suffers. The commonest type is similar to the fuse in a domestic plug, consisting of a short length of wire inside a glass tube. An increasingly common alternative is a small plastic peg with a strip of thin metal on the outside acting as the fuse. Both of these types have to be replaced completely when they 'blow'.

A circuit breaker is an automatic switch, which uses either the solenoid principle or the heating effect to switch itself off if the current flowing through it becomes dangerously high. They are more expensive than fuses, but you don't have to carry spares.

Fuses and circuit breakers occasionally 'blow' for no apparent reason. Although this is a nuisance, it's essential not to give in to the temptation to replace a fuse with a

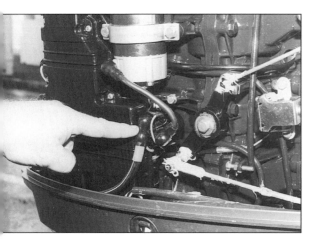

The starter solenoid is a remotely-controlled switch designed to handle the heavy current drawn by a starter motor.

bigger one, or to stop the breaker tripping with string or sticky tape! Find out why it's blowing, and cure the cause, rather than disabling your protection just when it's doing its job!

Solenoids

A **solenoid** consists of a coil of wire around a metal plunger. When electricity flows through the coil it becomes a magnet, and pulls the metal plunger into itself. This pulling action has all sorts of purposes on an engine: it can, for instance, be used as part of a remote control system allowing the choke to be operated electrically from a distance, or to operate the heavy duty switch that allows current to flow between the battery and starter motor.

. . . Things to do

Safety

Recoil starter springs are thin and springy: wear goggles and gloves when working on one, and be careful not to release it accidentally.

The low voltages used in boats' electrical systems are not inherently dangerous, but can still create heat or sparks that could start a fire. Use the isolator switch to disconnect the battery before working on or near the starter or alternator, and before physically disconnecting the battery terminals.

Never allow metal objects such as tools, jewellery, or watch straps to touch both terminals of a battery simultaneously. Ideally,

keep the terminals covered when working near a battery, and keep one terminal covered while you are working on the other.

Batteries give off explosive gases while being charged, so the battery compartment should be well ventilated, with the vent high up (to cope with gases that are lighter than air). Don't smoke near a battery, and avoid creating sparks.

Battery acid is highly corrosive. Use goggles and gloves, especially when cleaning battery terminals, and avoid spills. If you get splashed, use plenty of water to wash it off immediately.

. . . Things to do

Looking after your battery

All electrical connections need to be clean and tight, but one of the commonest causes of starting problems is corrosion around the battery terminals.

1 Slacken the clamp that secures the cables to the battery, and twist it to remove it from the terminal post. Flush off any white or cream-coloured 'fur' – acidic crystals of electrolyte – with plenty of very hot water before cleaning the terminals and posts with a wire brush or emery cloth.

2 Lightly smear the terminal posts with petroleum jelly, and wipe off any excess before replacing the terminal and tightening the clamp. Finally, smear the whole terminal with petroleum jelly to keep out moisture.

3 Over time, electrolysis and evaporation remove water from the battery, which has to be replaced by pouring distilled water into each cell of the battery until it just covers the top edges of the plates. Some modern batteries have specially-designed fillers intended to minimise the loss of electrolyte. Instructions for these are usually given on the battery casing.

4 If a battery is to be stored or left unused for more than a month or when there is any risk of freezing, it should be left disconnected and fully charged: a voltmeter connected between the + and - terminals should read no less than about 2.1 volts per cell, so a 6-cell, 12 volt battery should show at least 12.5 volts.

Replacing a starter cord

The most common problem associated with a recoil starter is a broken cord. This is cheap and easy to prevent by replacing the cord before it becomes unduly worn or frayed.

1 Remove the bolts (usually three) that hold the recoil starter assembly onto the engine.

2 Remove starter recoil housing.

3 If the starter cord is intact, pull it all the way out. Otherwise, turn the pulley by hand against the spring pressure, for about four turns.

4 Use a piece of wood, G-clamp, a pair of mole grips or a vise to stop the pulley turning.

5 Cut the old cord and release it from the handle and pulley.

6 Tie a knot in one end of the new cord, and thread the other end through the hole in the pulley and through the guide in the starter housing (use a piece of wire as a 'needle' if necessary). Pull it right through, and ensure that the knot is seated in the recess provided in the pulley.

7 Thread the other end of the cord through the handle, and tie a loose knot in the end.

8 Carefully release the clamping arrangement, to allow the spring to wind the cord into the starter.

9 Adjust the position of the knot at the handle end of the cord if necessary.

. . . Things to do

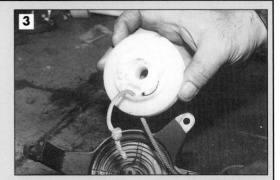

Replacing a starter spring

There are many different arrangements in use: in general, the spring is mounted above the pulley, between the pulley and the recoil starter housing. In the series of photos above, once the housing (**1**) has been removed, access to the spring is achieved by undoing a single screw or spring clip in the centre of the pulley (**2**). Be careful – this is when the spring may spring out!

Whether yours has the enclosed 'cartridge' type of spring or a loose spring, the general principle is to ensure that one end of the spring is located in a notch or peg either on the starter casing or on the stub axle that carries the pulley, while the other is located on a similar notch or peg on the pulley.

Photo **3** illustrates the under-side of the pulley showing the notch where the spring is going to locate. In photo **4** the pulley is about to be replaced (now correct way up) over the spring in the starter casing.

Once the spring is properly located, replace the screw or clip that secures the pulley in place.

. . . Things to do

Electrical maintenance and fault-finding

The majority of electrical problems are caused by poor connections or defective wiring, so fault-finding is made very much easier if you have a wiring diagram, and if the wires are either colour-coded or labelled.

A lot of preventative maintenance, however, involves no more than inspecting the visible wires and connections to make sure that connections are clean and tight and that the wires show no sign of fraying, breaking or corrosion. Look particularly carefully wherever the wires are free to move, or where they bend around a hard object such as the edge of a hole or duct. Having the right kind of wire helps enormously. 'Flex' made up of lots of thin strands is much less liable to break than 'cable' made up of one thick one, but matters can be improved still further by making sure the wires are well supported, and that where a wire emerges from a connector it is cushioned, stiffened and protected by a blob of silicon rubber sealant.

Don't be tempted to use electrical measuring equipment on an engine's electrics unless you know exactly what you are doing: some instruments (especially ohmmeters and 'meggers') produce sufficient electricity themselves to damage modern engine electrics if you apply the voltage in the wrong direction or mistakenly short circuit the wrong terminals.

8

Transmission

When you're concentrating on the engine itself, it's easy to forget that the object of the whole thing is to move the boat. To do so, the outboard needs a transmission system to convert the high-speed rotation of the engine's crankshaft into useful thrust from the propeller.

Of course, there are alternatives to propellers which may have advantages for specific applications, but propeller systems are good all-rounders that are reasonably cheap, simple, reliable, efficient, and easy to use.

They suffer, however, from one potentially significant drawback, which is that a small, fast-spinning propeller is generally less efficient than a larger one turning more slowly. Even on small pleasure craft, the optimum shaft speed is usually in the order of 1000rpm – less than a quarter of the speed of a typical outboard engine. Somehow, the shaft speed has to be reduced while its **torque** (turning effort) is increased.

It's also very useful to be able to reverse the direction of rotation, to provide astern power to stop the boat or make it go backwards, or to be able to fit counter-rotating propellers to a twin-screw boat.

A gearbox, then, may have to do three jobs:

- Reduce shaft speed

- Increase shaft torque

- Allow the direction of rotation to be selected

Gearboxes

The diagram (Fig 19) shows two gearwheels, whose teeth mesh together so that as one turns, the other has to turn as well. The smaller gear has 9 teeth, so if it is turning at 1000rpm, its teeth are moving at 9000 teeth per minute. The larger wheel is twice the size, and has 18 teeth, so although its teeth must also be moving at 9000 teeth per minute, that means only 500rpm. Notice, too, that if the smaller wheel is turning clockwise, the larger wheel must be turning anticlockwise.

Now imagine that you're using a spanner a foot long to turn the smaller wheel. If you apply an effort of 10lb to the end of the spanner, you're applying a torque of 10lbft (10lb at a radius of 1ft). The gearwheel is much smaller – let's say it has an effective radius of 1in. That means its teeth must be

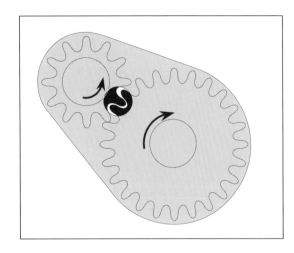

Fig 19 *The principle of a gearbox.*

pushing on the teeth of the other wheel with a force equivalent to 120lb. (120lb at a radius of $^1/_{12}$ft $= 120$ x $^1/_{12} = 10$lbft). The larger wheel has an effective radius of 2in, so a force of 120lb to its teeth corresponds to a torque of 20lbft (120 x $^2/_{12} =$ 20lbft).

In other words, by using a 9-tooth wheel to drive an 18-tooth wheel, we've:

- Halved the speed

- Doubled the torque

- Reversed the direction of rotation

Real gearboxes

Real gearboxes look more complicated, but depend on exactly this principle. In fact, the main difference between the simple gear train in Fig 19 and the gearbox shown in Fig 20 is that the gearbox uses cone-shaped bevel gears, so that although the shaft coming down from the engine is vertical, its output shaft is horizontal.

The other obvious difference is that there are more gears involved. This is to provide a choice of ahead or astern gear.

The bevel gear on the input shaft turns

two slightly larger bevel gears that spin freely on the horizontal shaft. They are the same size as each other so they turn at the same speed, but as one is driven by the forward edge of the input gear and the other by the rear edge, they rotate in opposite directions.

Between the two gears is a sliding clutch assembly, roughly cylindrical in shape, but with its ends carved into a pattern of sloping steps. Ridges called **splines** on the shaft and matching grooves in the clutch ensure that although it can easily slide along the shaft, it can't turn without turning the shaft as well. Moving the gear lever slides the clutch along the shaft so that the steps on one end fit into a matching pattern of steps in one of the spinning gears, locking that gear onto the shaft and forcing the shaft to spin with it.

Propellers

Compared with the myriad components that make up an engine, a propeller looks extremely simple. It's certainly true that there is little that can go wrong with a propeller, apart from physical damage such as bent, chipped or broken blades, but the science of propellers is remarkably complicated, and it's worth being sure that you've got the right propeller for the job: it needs to be carefully matched to the boat, engine, and gearbox.

You can think of a propeller in any of three ways:

- As a screw

- As a pump

- As a foil

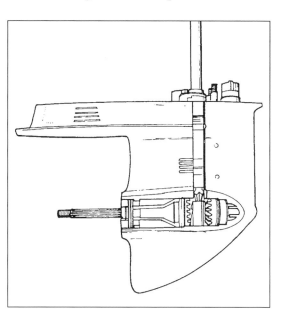

Fig 20 *A typical gearbox. By courtesy of Clymer Publications, a division of Intertec Publishing.*

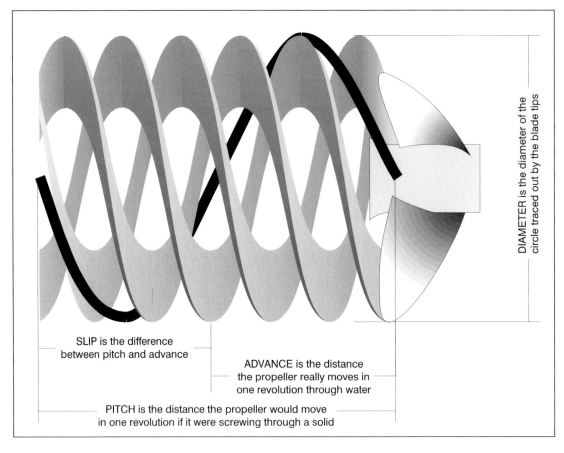

SLIP is the difference between pitch and advance

ADVANCE is the distance the propeller really moves in one revolution through water

PITCH is the distance the propeller would move in one revolution if it were screwing through a solid

DIAMETER is the diameter of the circle traced out by the blade tips

Fig 21 *Propeller terminology.*

None of them tells the whole story, but between them they provide a working knowledge of a subject which could easily fill several books each much bigger than this one.

The propeller as a screw

One theory regards the propeller as a screw, winding its way through the water like a bolt winding its way into a nut. It is not a very good theory, because a propeller does not work in a solid medium, but it explains some of the terminology.

Pitch is the distance the propeller would move in one revolution if it were screwing its way through a solid. In practice it does not move quite that far: the distance it really moves is the **advance**. The difference between pitch and advance is the **slip**.

The picture is complicated by the fact that the advance isn't quite the same as the distance the boat moves: for one thing the boat tends to drag some water along with it, and for another, the water directly affected by the propeller tends to move astern compared with the water nearby. This makes it very difficult to measure the true slip. It's very much easier to find the **apparent slip**, which is the difference between the boat's movement and the pitch. For high performance planing boats, the apparent slip may be 10% of the pitch or even less, but for a heavy motor-sailer or workboat it can be as much as 50%.

The propeller as a pump

Another theory treats the propeller as a pump, squirting water backwards. Newton's third law of motion says that for every action there is an equal but opposite reaction, so if the propeller pushes a lump of water backwards, the water also pushes the propeller (and the boat to which it is attached) forwards.

The amount of water the propeller can push in a given time depends mainly on the power available: a 10hp engine, for instance, can move about 5 cubic feet per second. You can think of that 5ft^3 of water as being in the shape of a cylinder, whose diameter is roughly the same as that of the propeller, and whose length is roughly the distance the prop has moved through the water in the time. For a slow boat, moving at 10 feet per second, that means the cylinder must have a cross-section of 0.5ft^2 or a diameter of about $9^1/2$ inches. For a lightweight inflatable, doing perhaps 25 feet per

second with the same engine, the cylinder's cross section must be reduced to 0.2ft^2, or about 6inches in diameter.

This suggests – correctly – that the diameter of a propeller should vary depending on the power transmitted (because that determines the volume of water it can move in one second) and the speed at which the boat is moving (because that determines the length of the cylinder).

The propeller as a foil

A more recent, realistic, and complicated theory regards each blade of the propeller as a foil, like a boat's sail or an aircraft's wing.

Like a sail, the blade has to be at a slight angle to the fluid flowing over it if it is to generate any useful force. Unfortunately, increasing this **angle of attack** doesn't just increase the useful thrust: it also increases the drag – which is one of the reasons why over-sheeting a sail makes it less efficient.

For a sail, the optimum angle between the sail and the airflow is about 20°–25°, but for a propeller blade in water it is much smaller – about 4°.

The analogy with sailing goes on if you think about how the flow across the propeller blade is created. The 'apparent wind' flowing across a sail is made up of two components: the 'true wind' that would be felt if the boat were stationary, and the 'induced wind' caused by its own movement through the air. In the case of a propeller blade, the equivalent of the true wind is created by the rotation of the propeller, while its 'induced wind' is caused by its movement through the water.

That is why a propeller blade needs to be twisted: 'induced wind' is much the same all over the propeller, but the 'true wind' varies dramatically, because the tip of each blade sweeps around a much bigger circle than the sections of the blade that are nearer the shaft.

It also suggests that the pitch of the

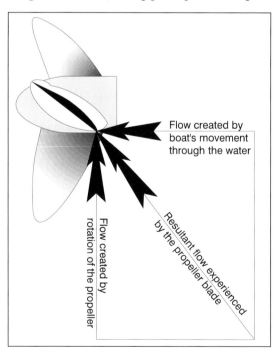

Flow created by boat's movement through the water

Flow created by rotation of the propeller

Resultant flow experienced by the propeller blade

Fig 22 *Water flow over a propeller.*

propeller needs to be carefully matched to the speed at which the water is moving through the propeller: a fast boat generally needs much more pitch than a slow one, in order to cope with the much greater 'induced wind'.

Choosing a propeller

What all this boils down to is that the choice of propeller depends on a mass of interrelated variables that include:

- The power available

- The shaft speed

- The speed of the propeller through the water

There are so many variables (even the temperature and salinity of the water have a part to play) that trying to work out the pitch and diameter of the ideal propeller for a particular boat from pure theory is almost impossible. It's important to pick the right one, though, because the wrong propeller

can easily make a big difference to the boat's performance.

Fortunately, although engines are usually supplied with a 'standard' propeller, outboard manufacturers recognise the significance of propeller choice, and offer a range of alternatives. Don't be afraid to seek advice from the engine dealer about which will suit your purposes.

Cavitation and ventilation

Although the words 'cavitation' and 'ventilation' are often used interchangeably, they

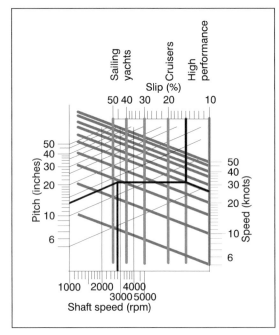

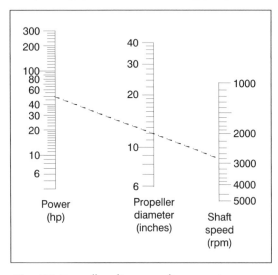

Fig 23 Propeller diameter diagram. Lay a straight edge across the two known variables to find the unknown.

For example, for 50hp delivered through a shaft turning at 2800rpm, the optimum diameter is approximately 12in.

Fig 24 Propeller pitch diagram. First estimate a likely value for slip. From this figure on the top scale, drop vertically to meet the diagonal corresponding to your estimated speed.

From that intersection, draw a horizontal line to meet the vertical drawn upwards from the shaft speed on the bottom scale. Where these two meet gives the optimum pitch.

For example, for a RIB expected to achieve 25 knots with a 50hp engine, and a shaft speed of 2800rpm, the optimum pitch is approximately 13in.

are really two quite different things. What they have in common is that they can rob a propeller of almost all its grip on the water.

Ventilation is most common on sports boats and on sailing boats with outboard motors mounted high on their transoms, because it is caused by air being sucked into the propeller. A propeller designed to operate in water obviously can't work very well in air: it generates very little thrust and suffers very little drag, so the engine speed increases while the boat slows down.

Manufacturers minimise the risk of ventilation by incorporating an anti-ventilation plate (often called a 'cavitation plate') in the drive leg, just above the propeller, but if this is not enough, then you may need to consider either lowering the engine or moderating your driving style!

Cavitation is caused by the propeller itself. As it rotates, it creates thrust by increasing the pressure on the aft faces of its blades and simultaneously reducing the pressure on their forward faces. As the pressure falls, the boiling point of water reduces, eventually reaching the stage at which it will boil even at sea temperature. When this happens, bubbles of water vapour form on the forward face of the propeller. The immediate effect of severe cavitation is very much like that of ventilation: the engine races but the propeller ceases to generate much thrust. The long-term effect of even minor cavitation is an erosion of the propeller blades known as 'cavitation burn', caused by the collapsing bubbles.

Cavitation can be caused by using the wrong propeller for the boat, such as one with too much pitch or not enough blade area, but can also be caused by damage to the propeller such as nicks in the leading edge of the blade.

When cavitation strikes, the immediate cure is to throttle back until the propeller regains its 'bite' on solid water. In the longer term, if your propeller is prone to

cavitation, you may need to change it for one which has more blades or bigger blades.

Propeller hubs

One of the weakest links in the transmission system is between the propeller and its shaft. That is quite deliberate: if the two were rigidly locked together and the propeller hit an obstruction, it would damage itself severely, and send shock loads up through the transmission system which might cause serious damage to the engine itself. There are two main ways of providing this 'weak link'.

Shear pins

Many small outboards use a very simple arrangement known as a **shear pin**. The propeller shaft is smooth, as is the hole in the middle of the propeller. What holds the two together is a metal pin, about an inch or so long, which passes through a hole in the shaft. When the propeller is slid onto the shaft, notches in its hub fit over the pin so that it has to turn with the shaft.

Unfortunately, shear pins are prone to metal fatigue and can shear for no apparent reason, so it is wise to carry a spare (often supplied with the engine, held in a clip inside the cowling).

Splined hubs

Larger outboards – and some small ones – have splines (longitudinal ridges) along their propeller shafts which match up with splines inside the hub of the propeller. To provide the 'weak link', however, the splined hub is not rigidly attached to the propeller itself, but is separated from it by a rubber bush.

This is less likely to fail than a shear pin, but after considerable use it is quite possible for the rubber bush to start to slip inside the propeller hub, and when it does so it will quickly wear itself away until all drive is lost.

. . . Things to do

Safety

A spinning propeller on an engine that has accidentally been started ashore is extremely dangerous. Do not attempt to remove a propeller without first disabling the engine – ideally by disconnecting the spark plug leads.

Changing a propeller or shear pin

To make sure that the propeller does not seize onto the shaft, it is a good idea to remove it at least once a year, and to coat the shaft with non-graphite grease. This is also an opportunity to clear any fishing line or bits of string from around the shaft, which might otherwise damage the seal that keeps oil inside the gearbox and water out.

1 Straighten the legs of the split pin or tab washer that hold the propeller nut in place and remove.

2 Undo the propeller nut, and remove it.

3 Remove washers, noting their positions.

4 Slide the propeller off the shaft. Again, note the position of any washers, springs, or line-cutters fitted between the propeller and gearbox.

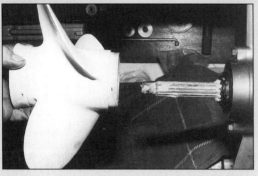

To change a propeller, first remove the split pin that holds the propeller nut in place (top), then remove the nut (second from top) and any washers, being sure to note which order the washers come off (second from bottom). The propeller should then slide off easily. Remove any weed or fishing line from the shaft before greasing it ready to refit the propeller (bottom).

5 Remove any debris from around the shaft, and any pieces of broken shear pin trapped in the hole in the shaft or in the propeller.

6 Grease the shaft and reassemble, using a new shear pin if necessary.

7 Tighten the propeller nut, ideally using a torque wrench set to the manufacturer's recommendations. On small engines (up to about 40hp) it is easy to overtighten.

8 Replace the split pin locking the propeller nut in place, or bend up the legs of the tab washer.

Looking after your gearbox
Apart from regular oil changes and inspection, a gearbox needs very little attention. The best thing you can do to ensure that it stays in good condition is to make sure that anyone operating the boat develops driving habits that don't inflict damage to it. This means:

- Allowing the engine speed to drop to tick-over before engaging or changing gear.

- Changing gear positively. Don't be hesitant or unduly cautious, as this produces a chattering noise that is caused by the teeth of the clutch knocking bits off their counterparts on the gears.

9

Control Systems

You don't have to move far up the scale of outboard-powered craft to find some kind of remote control system.

As is often the case on boats, there is no 'standard' arrangement: push-pull cables are by far the commonest, but even these are available in several different forms and face competition from hydraulic systems and electronics.

Throttle and gear controls

The cables that are used in most remote control systems are rather like those that work the brakes on a bicycle, with a central control cable inside a tubular outer casing. The casing is fixed at both ends, so that when you pull one end of the inner cable, the other end retracts.

Boats' control cables are usually very much bigger and more robust than those on a push-bike, but the main difference is that instead of using very flexible multi-strand wire for the inner cable, marine systems use a single strand of stiff wire so that they can push as well as pull.

Control heads

It's easy to see how cables can be used in a twin-lever system, where one lever controls the engine and another operates the gearbox. Pushing the top of the 'throttle' lever forwards, for instance, pulls on the cable, which in turn pulls the linkage that opens the throttle on the engine.

Single-lever systems, in which the engine and gearbox are both controlled by the same lever, are generally more popular but

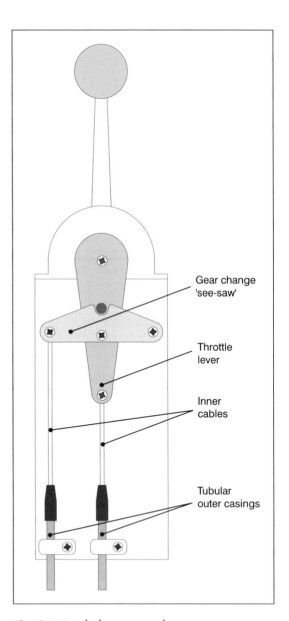

Fig 25 *Single-lever control unit.*

Gear change 'see-saw'

Throttle lever

Inner cables

Tubular outer casings

are more complicated because they have to achieve a positive gear shift between ahead, neutral, and astern but also offer progressive control of the engine speed.

This is achieved by connecting the throttle cable directly to the control lever, while the gear cable is connected to a horizontal see-saw arrangement. A peg sticking out of the throttle lever engages in a notch in the top edge of the see-saw, so that the first few degrees of movement of the control lever is enough to rock the see-saw so that it pulls or pushes on the gear cable. The geometry of the arrangement is such that this first movement of the control lever has virtually no effect on the throttle cable. Once the see-saw has been rocked far enough to engage gear, however, the peg is clear of the slot, and the lever can move further, pulling on the throttle cable without having any more effect on the gear control linkage.

Cables
Cable systems are generally reliable so long as they are properly installed in the first place and then receive a certain minimal level of maintenance. It's worth doing, because if your control system fails, you will almost certainly look foolish (bystanders never believe that a messed up manoeuvre was caused by mechanical problems), and you may well face serious damage or injury.

When problems do occur, control failure is more often due to problems with the cable, rather than to the control units themselves:

- Internal corrosion, caused by water getting in through splits in the outer cable, can jam the inner cable.

- Wear on the inner surfaces of the outer cable allows the inner cable to slop from side to side producing excessive backlash (free play) on the cable end: on a gear cable this may mean that there is not enough controlled movement to operate the gear lever properly.

- Bent or corroded end rods make operation stiff and may eventually lead to the inner cable stretching; again, this is particularly serious in the gear cable.

- Worn, corroded, or disconnected end fittings. The split pins that secure the cable to the gearbox and fuel pump are so thin that they are particularly prone to corrosion, but look out, too, for the clamping arrangements that hold the outer cable in place.

- Poorly-designed cable runs can make controls stiff from the outset, and give rise to a lot of backlash. Over time, this gets worse, as the bends cause increased wear and tear inside the cable: ideally cables should be dead straight, with no long sweeping bends or bends tighter than about 8in (20cm) radius.

Steering controls

Wire steering
Wire steering uses the steering wheel to turn a drum containing several turns of flexible wire so that turning the drum reels in one end of the wire and lets out the other. The two ends are routed around the boat on pulleys, and hooked onto the steering bar at the front of the engine.

Wire steering is simple – one might almost say 'primitive' – but reasonably effective and reliable. Its main drawbacks are that it tends to have a sloppy response (caused by free play in the system), its appearance, and the wear and tear on the wire. Problems most often arise by the wire jumping off the pulleys or, more seriously, by the pulleys coming away from their mountings.

It is important to appreciate that the steering pulleys can be under very heavy loads, so they need to be through-bolted to a substantial part of the boat's structure. It is a good idea to incorporate a bottle screw (tensioner) in the longest run of wire on one side so that the tension can be adjusted, and a spring in the other side to allow the motor to be tilted without having to disconnect the steering.

Cable steering

Cable steering systems use what are in effect enlarged versions of throttle and gear cables to push and pull the outboard's steering bar.

The steering wheel turns the input shaft of a simple gearbox, usually mounted out of sight behind the console, which reduces several turns of the steering wheel to a single turn of the output gear. Instead of turning a shaft, however, the output gear has the steering cable locked to its edge, so that as it turns, it either pushes or pulls on the inner cable.

At the other end, the outer cable is usually clamped to the engine's tilt pivot. A rigid extension of the inner cable extends from it, with another bar connecting the end of this to the engine. Pivots, or ball and socket joints, allow the motor to be tilted.

Hydraulic steering

Hydraulic steering systems use a similar linkage at the motor end, except that instead of using a cable to do the pushing and pulling, they have a hydraulic ram clamped to the tilt pivot.

The steering wheel turns the input shaft of a hydraulic pump, which pumps oil through the pipe work and into one end of the ram, while receiving excess oil from the other end.

Hydraulic steering systems are expensive, but are rugged and reliable so long as they are kept topped up with clean hydraulic fluid. They virtually eliminate any 'feel' the driver gets from the steering system, and can easily be adapted to suit an autopilot.

Trim and tilt systems

The performance of an outboard-powered boat can be radically altered by changing

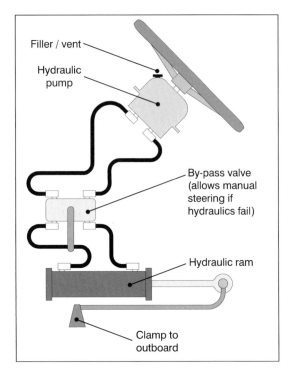

Fig. 26 *Hydraulic steering system.*

Labels: Filler / vent; Hydraulic pump; By-pass valve (allows manual steering if hydraulics fail); Hydraulic ram; Clamp to outboard

the angle of the thrust from the motor. On simple motors, this can only be achieved when the engine is switched off, but many motors over about 30hp have a facility called power trim, which uses hydraulics to adjust the angle of the motor whilst under way.

As with most such refinements, there are significant differences between one make and model and another which make it unwise to tamper with the hydraulic tilt system without referring to the manufacturer's manual.

The principle, however, is that a rocker switch on the boat's console is used to operate one or the other of two solenoids, which supply power to an electrically-driven hydraulic pump. The pump, in turn, supplies pressurised hydraulic fluid to a two-way ram, which trims the motor in or out, depending on which end is receiving the supply from the pump.

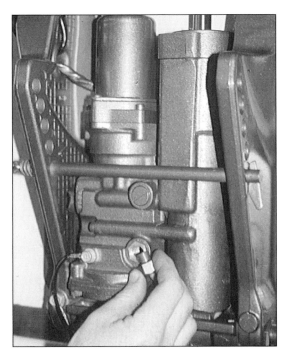

Of course, it takes more effort to trim the motor out against the thrust of the propeller, so some systems use two extra one-way rams to trim the motor out.

Key safety features of all hydraulic tilt mechanisms are a safety valve, built into the system to allow the engine to kick up if the leg hits an obstruction, and a by-pass valve that allows the hydraulic fluid to flow freely from one end of the ram to the other so that the motor can be tilted by hand if the hydraulic system fails.

Hydraulic trim and tilt allows the angle of the engine's thrust to be optimised for different conditions. Different systems vary, so be sure to consult the manual before working on it, as it may contain oil under high pressure. To check the fluid level of a power trim and tilt system, always raise the leg to its maximum height. Photo: Philip Pond

. . . Things to do

Safety
A large outboard is a heavy piece of equipment; do not tinker with hydraulic tilt or trim systems without referring to the manufacturer's instructions, as the system may be under considerable pressure.

Control cables

- Once or twice a season, inspect the cable end fittings for wear and corrosion. Replace split pins with new ones if they are corroded, or if they have been removed for any reason.

- With the inner cable in its fully extended position, lightly grease the exposed part with a non-graphite grease.

- Clean and re-grease the moving parts of control heads.

- Inspect the cable run, looking for splits or wear in the outer plastic sheath – often given away by rust streaks.

Wire steering systems

- Once a season, inspect the wire looking for worn or broken strands. If you are using unsheathed wire, clean it with a de-greasing agent such as Jizer or Gunk, and apply a fresh coat of non-graphite grease.

- Check the pulleys to make sure they are securely attached to the boat and turn freely.

- If necessary, tighten the adjuster to take up any slack caused by the cable stretching or by wear and tear, to make sure that the cable cannot jump off the pulleys.

Cable steering systems
Steering cables require much the same maintenance as throttle and gear cables. A common problem, however, arises from corrosion between the push rod at the motor end of the cable and the motor's tilt pivot. This can be minimised by making sure to turn the wheel from 'lock to lock' a few times every month, and by making sure that the rod is kept greased.

When leaving the boat, it is best to make sure the steering is left with the rod in its fully extended position: it is slightly more vulnerable to corrosion in that position, but is almost infinitely easier to release if corrosion occurs.

Hydraulic steering
A hydraulic steering system should normally be left with its ram fully retracted, so that the oil in the ram protects the push-rod against corrosion.

Other than guarding against the risk of corrosion, the other main maintenance task is to ensure that the system is kept topped up with hydraulic fluid. Some systems have a separate reservoir; others store fluid in the pump unit.

If the system becomes noisy or lacks response, it may be because there is air in the system. Sometimes this can be cleared by topping up the reservoir and then winding the steering from lock to lock a few times with the filler cap off, but it is best to follow the manufacturer's instructions if possible.

10

Tools and Working Practices

A lot of work on an engine involves removing and replacing components, so it involves dealing with a wide variety of fastenings – literally, 'getting down to the nuts and bolts'.

Nuts and bolts

Bolts vary in length and diameter, but come in a number of standard sizes quoted in imperial or metric measurements. Metric measurements are now used almost universally on British, European and Japanese equipment while Imperial sizes are found on old British equipment and on almost anything intended primarily for the American market. This means that you are unlikely to come across a mixture of the two on one engine, but doesn't mean to say that you won't find Imperial fastenings on the engine and metric elsewhere on the boat – or vice versa.

Even if you find two bolts of exactly the same diameter, they may not be interchangeable because there are a variety of different 'standard' screw threads which differ in cross section as well as in the number of threads per inch (Fig 27). It's important to make sure that you match the right nut and bolt together and that you screw bolts or studs back into the holes they came out of because although some odd combinations are compatible, the vast majority are not. Unless a nut or bolt is clearly in poor condition, it should turn smoothly and easily until it reaches the final tightening up stage: if it starts easily but suddenly becomes stiff for no obvious reason, or if it

feels unusually floppy, it's a pretty fair bet that it's the wrong one for the job.

If the differences between screw threads seem subtle, the differences between their heads certainly are not: it is obvious that you can't use a spanner to undo a bolt with a domed and slotted head intended for a screwdriver! It's surprising, though, how often DIY mechanics find themselves trying to work with spanners or screwdrivers that don't quite fit. It's important to use the right tool for the job because – although a 13mm spanner will just about cope with a 1/2in hexagon head – it is slightly too large. The difference is only about a quarter of a

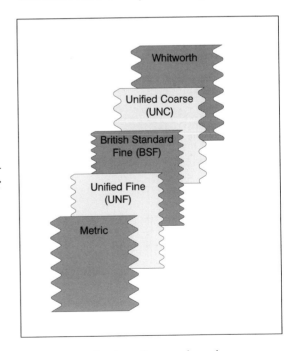

Fig 27 A selection of screw threads.

millimetre, but that is enough to allow the nut to twist between the jaws. Instead of the load being spread across the flats of the nut, it is then concentrated at the corners, so as soon as you try to apply any appreciable force to the spanner, the nut levers the jaws of the spanner apart, while the spanner rounds off the corners of the nut.

Similar comments apply to screwdrivers – probably the most misused tools of all. Not only do you need the right kind of screwdriver – flat-bladed for slotted heads, and cross-point for cross-heads – but it should also be the right size for the job. A screwdriver which is too big won't go into the slot at all, but one which is too small will tend to twist out of shape and damage the edges of the slot. A flat-bladed screwdriver should be ground to a fairly shallow taper, so that it doesn't try to lever itself out of the slot, and have a sharp-edged square tip so that it doesn't hit the bottom of the slot before it makes contact with the sides.

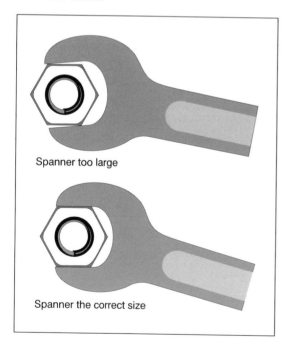

Spanner too large

Spanner the correct size

Fig 28 *Use a spanner that fits!*

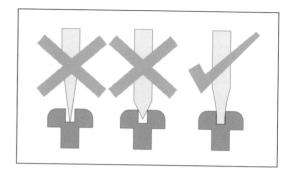

Fig 29 *Use a screwdriver that fits!*

Allen screws

The drive towards more compact engines has made engine manufacturers turn increasingly to fastenings with 'unconventional' heads. Allen screws, in which the head of the bolt has a hexagonal recess, are now so common that they hardly rank as unconventional. Dealing with these needs either a screwdriver equipped with a selection of appropriate 'bits' or a set of Allen keys – bent pieces of hexagonal hardened steel bar. You may need lots of them: Allen screws come in a variety of metric and Imperial sizes, and a good fit between the tool and the fastening is even more important than for a spanner – not least because if you damage the head of an Allen screw it can be exceedingly difficult to remove.

Locking devices

Some fastenings are used in applications where they are particularly likely to come undone, or in circumstances where their failure would be catastrophic. To overcome this, they may be fitted with one of a number of locking devices.

Shake-proof washers have teeth cut into their inner or outer edges, to provide extra grip between the nut or bolt and the part it is holding. Internal shake-proof washers should be used under the heads of bolts, while external shake-proof washers go under nuts.

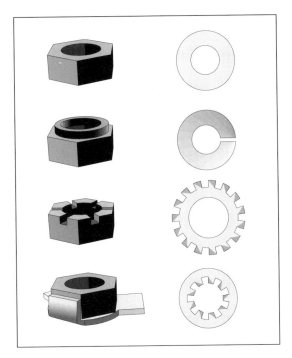

Fig 30 *Locking devices. Left (from top): plain nut, self-locking nut, castellated nut, tab washer. Right (from top): plain washer, spring washer, external shake-proof washer, internal shake-proof washer.*

Self-locking nuts, often known by the brand name 'Nyloc', have plastic inserts in their tops. The insert is slightly smaller than the diameter of the corresponding bolt, which has to cut its own thread into the plastic producing a locking effect. Ideally, a self-locking nut should only be used once, but you can rejuvenate one if necessary by crimping the head down to expand the plastic before it is re-fitted.

Tab washers have flaps or tabs which fold up to grip the sides of the nut. When fitting a tab washer, it is a good plan to bend the tabs up slightly before tightening the nut, as this makes it easier to bend them right up later. Tab washers can be re-used, but you should avoid using the same tab more than

once, as it will eventually break off due to metal fatigue.

Castellated nuts, sometimes called **crown nuts**, have a ring of deep notches cut in the top. A split pin passes through a hole in the bolt or shaft and through the notches to stop the nut turning. A castellated cap, which fits over a conventional nut, may sometimes be used to achieve the same effect. Split pins should only be used once, and should have their legs fully opened out.

Pipe fittings

Pipe fittings, too, come in a variety of shapes and sizes, designed to cope with pipes of different materials and different sizes, and with operating pressures ranging from partial vacuum to several thousand pounds per square inch. There are, however, only three main types that you are likely to come across.

Pipe clips

Pipe clips are bands of thin metal designed to fit round flexible pipes. The most common type, often known by the brand name 'Jubilee clip', has a bolt or screw joining the ends of the band so that it can be tightened to compress the pipe against the rigid spigot to which it is attached. An alternative consists of a ring of metal with small bulges that can be squeezed with pliers to reduce the effective diameter of the clip. They're found in all sorts of relatively low pressure applications, from marine toilets to engine cooling systems and exhaust pipes.

Removing a screwed hose clip is a simple matter of unscrewing the clip until it is loose enough to slide along the hose and then pulling the hose off the spigot. In practice, a common problem is that the hose may have glued itself to the spigot, in which case it may come free if you massage the hose to loosen the bond, and then prise it off with a screwdriver. As a last resort, a flexible pipe can always be cut, but do make sure you have a replacement available before you do so. Crimped on clips may be worked loose with a spike or an old screwdriver; if this does not work, they have to be cut off.

Replacing a hose can be more difficult, because it may be such a tight fit on the spigot that you wonder why it needs a hose clip at all. Dipping the end of the hose in boiling water may help by softening it, and a smear of washing-up liquid can be used to provide some gentle lubrication. Whatever method you use, it's worth threading the pipe clip onto the hose first, so that you don't have to unscrew it completely in order to fit it onto the pipe in situ.

Fitting the pipe onto the spigot is especially difficult if the spigot has a bulge or ridge around its end, but these things are not put there just to make life difficult; they are intended to provide extra security once the pipe is in place. They only work, however, if you make sure that the hose clip is on the right side of the ridge – nearest the root of the spigot so that the pipe would have to drag the pipe clip over the ridge in order to pull itself free.

Compression fittings
Compression fittings are used on rigid pipes, or occasionally on flexible pipes with a rigid insert. There are two types, but both look like an unusually deep nut with the pipe sticking out of the middle.

One kind, used mainly on relatively low pressure applications such as domestic plumbing and sometimes on the low pressure side of the fuel system, uses a straight-ended pipe with a brass or plastic ring called an **olive** threaded onto it. The end of the pipe fits into a recess in the spigot, but the olive rests on top. Then, when the nut is tightened down onto the threaded spigot, the olive is compressed between the 'nut' and the spigot, to grip the pipe and form the seal.

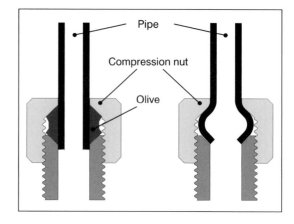

Fig 31 *Pipe fittings.*

The only cause for concern when working with this type of pipe fitting is that over-tightening it can distort or split the olive.

High pressure pipes use a development of this principle in which the pipe itself is shaped to form the olive. Making the joint in the first place requires special equipment, but once the pipe has been shaped it forms a secure and leak-proof joint that is as easy to do up or undo as a nut and bolt. Perhaps the biggest danger is the temptation to treat these kinds of joint as though they are flexible: they're not, so don't try to bend or move the pipe without slackening the unions that hold it in place.

Banjo bolts
The third kind of pipe union is called a **banjo bolt** – so called because one part of it is supposed to look like a banjo. The 'banjo' is a metal fitting that has to be brazed or soldered onto the pipe, and which then forms a hollow channel right around the central bolt. The 'bolt' part looks exactly like a conventional bolt, except that its head is often rather larger and thinner than you might expect, and its shaft is a hollow. A hole in the side of the bolt allows liquid to flow from the pipe, around the circular channel formed by the banjo, and down through the hollow bolt.

Brass, fibre, or nylon washers form a seal around the upper and lower edges of the banjo to stop leaks: be careful not to lose them when undoing a banjo bolt, and make sure that they go back when you replace it.

Seals and gaskets

Other joints in an engine, such as those between the cylinder block and the cylinder head, are just as important as the joints in the 'plumbing' that surrounds it. It's difficult to get a good metal to metal seal over a wide area, especially as the parts concerned may be expanding and contracting at different rates when the engine warms up and cools down. To overcome the problem, these kinds of joint usually include a **gasket** of more resilient material.

Some gaskets, especially cylinder head gaskets, are quite sophisticated components in their own right, including layers of different materials and inserts to withstand particular stresses or to help them stay in shape, but the majority of gaskets are relatively simple sheets of steel, copper, cork, rubber or paper.

Copper gaskets are used in small, highly stressed joints, and usually look much like ordinary washers. Ideally, a copper gasket should only be used once, because it loses its resilience once it has been fitted. If necessary, though, it can be renovated by heating it over a gas ring until it turns blue, and then immediately dropping it into cold water.

At the other extreme are **cork** or **rubber gaskets** used in places where there are no great stresses involved, but the possibility of considerable movement, or where the parts concerned are so delicate that they would distort if they were bolted down too firmly. The only snag with these is that the gasket almost invariably sticks to one or the other of the two components: if part of it sticks to one and the rest of it sticks to the other, you may need to peel it away very carefully

with a thin knife to make sure it comes away in one piece.

Paper gaskets are less resilient than cork or rubber, but they work well and are so cheap that although it's almost impossible to salvage one once it has been used, there is no excuse for not using a new one every time. If you can not get a ready-made replacement, it is easy to make your own from a sheet of gasket paper. In a real emergency, it is even possible to use writing paper or a cornflake packet for a gasket as a stopgap!

The first step in the process of replacing a gasket is to remove all traces of the old gasket from the surfaces. You may need to use a scraper, but be careful not to scratch the machined surfaces – If you must use a screwdriver for the job, file the corners off first!

Then, if you're making a new paper gasket, smear one of the mating surfaces with a little oil, and press it down hard onto the gasket paper so as to leave a clear picture of its shape and any holes that are needed.

Once you've cut out the new gasket, use another smear of oil to stick it temporarily to one surface, and make future separation of the joint easier. Then reassemble the joint and tighten all the bolts evenly.

Tools

The standard advice about tools is to 'buy the best you can afford'. All too often that advice goes with a list of 'essential' tools and spares that would not disgrace a professional workshop, but would go a long way towards sinking a RIB or a small cruising yacht!

There is no doubt that high-quality, high price tools such as those made by Britool, Gedore, and Snap-On are virtually indestructible and a pleasure to use, but unfortunately they sink just as quickly as any others if they get dropped overboard, rust nearly as quickly once they've been exposed to salt water, and are exceptionally prone to being 'borrowed'.

Very cheap tools, such as many of those imported from India and China, will let you believe you've got a full tool kit until you try unscrewing a tough nut in an awkward spot. That's when you find out that the reason they are cheaper is because they do not fit as well as they should do in the first place, and that they get worse once they start to bend under the strain.

Fortunately there are plenty of mid-range tools made by companies such as Stanley and Kamasa, which are nearly as good as the front-runners but are a fraction of the price.

Tricks of the trade

The possibility that you might take an engine to pieces and not be able to put it back together again is probably the mechanic's worst nightmare. The best tip for avoiding it is to be scrupulously and relentlessly methodical: lay the bits of your engine down in the order they were removed, and keep the fastenings with the relevant part – do not tip all the nuts and bolts into one box, because it may then take hours of trial and error to find the right one – and do not complicate matters by taking things apart unnecessarily.

It almost goes without saying that you should refer to the manual for any job that is not completely familiar to you, but if you do find yourself working without a manual, do not be afraid to make notes or sketches of the order in which things came apart or what went where. Look carefully at any component before you remove it, and try to figure out what it does, which bolts hold it on, and which hold something inside it.

Seized fastenings

Seized fastenings make life difficult, but are a common feature of many boat engines. Before applying brute force, it is important

As any mechanic will tell you, it is essential to have the correct tool for the job. Photo: Philip Pond.

to bear in mind that conventional spanners are designed to apply the right amount of leverage for the fastenings they fit, and that if you lengthen a spanner to unscrew a bolt that is already weakened by corrosion, you may make it shear off completely. The first stage is to make sure that you are working efficiently:

- Try to give yourself as much room and light as you need.

- Keep your hands and tools clean so that you can get a good grip.

- Pull on the end of a spanner rather than pushing it: you are less likely to get hurt if the spanner slips, and applying force at the end instead of the middle gives you more leverage.

- Use a ring spanner if possible, rather than an open-ended one.

- Turn the nut rather than the bolt.

If none of these do the trick, it is worth trying to tighten the offending fastening to break the bond between the threads, and penetrating oil can work wonders so long as it is left alone for long enough to penetrate.

More drastic measures include lengthening the spanner with a length of pipe, and shock treatment by tapping the spanner with a hammer while applying steady pressure by hand.

For a really stubborn fastening, you may have to resort to more destructive methods such as using a cold chisel or a gadget called a nut splitter (like an oversized ring spanner, but with a blade which can be screwed in to break a seized nut) to split the nut, or a hacksaw to cut the side off it. Bolt heads that have rounded off can be carefully filed down to take the next size of spanner, or can have a slot hacksawed in. Most drastic of all, but often quickest, is to cut through the bolt completely.

Destroying a nut and bolt is not too frightening because it can always be replaced, but the idea of cutting or snapping a stud or bolt that has seized into a casting is more worrying. Even so, it is not the end of the world.

Once the load has been removed from the broken stud, it may unscrew relatively easily, particularly if it has been well soaked with penetrating oil. This is where mole grips come in handy. Alternatively, you could try cutting a screwdriver slot in the remains, or screwing two nuts down onto it. Once the second nut has been tightened down hard against the first, a spanner applied to the lower nut can be used to unscrew the stud.

If the stud has broken off flush with the casting, it should be possible to drill a hole down the centre of it in order to use a tool called a **stud extractor**. This is a tapered rod of hardened steel with a very coarse thread cut into it. The stud extractor's thread is in the opposite direction to that of a conventional bolt, so as you screw the stud extractor into the stud, it first grips the side of the drilled hole, and then unscrews the stud.

If this does not work, it may be possible to drill out the stud altogether, and then use a device called a **tap** to recut the thread in the hole. Taps, unfortunately, are quite expensive, so it is hardly worth having a full set in hand to cope with the occasional mishap, so it may be worth referring the job to a professional.

The ultimate sanction is definitely a professional's job because of the equipment required, but it is worth knowing that it is possible to drill out the hole oversize, and put in a completely new thread known as a **helicoil insert**.

Tool Kit

Open-ended spanners, a set of the right sizes – Imperial (AF) or metric – is essential, and if you have a very old boat or engine, you may need the now obsolete Whitworth sizes, too.

Ring spanners are better if you need to use much force or work in an awkward position, but can't be used on pipe fittings or lock nuts. As you need two spanners of the same size to undo a nut and bolt anyway, it makes sense to have one set of rings and one of open-ended.

Combination spanners have a ring on one end and an open-ended on the other but as both ends are usually the same size, you will still need two sets!

Socket spanners make life much easier, and are the only way of getting at some of the less accessible fastenings on compact modern engines, but it's debatable whether they are essential for basic maintenance. They're nice to have, and the $1/4$in drive socket sets that best suit the small fastenings used on many outboards are relatively economical, but they are no substitute for conventional spanners because there are some fastenings they cannot cope with. Whitworth socket spanners are very hard to come by, but a set of tubular box spanners is a reasonable alternative.

Spark plug spanner. This no longer deserves pride of place in an outboard mechanic's tool kit, but is worth having because a proper plug spanner is less likely to damage the plug than any alternative. You will only need one, so long as you get the right size, but it is pointless having a plug spanner unless you have a set of **feeler gauges** or a **spark plug adjusting tool** to go with it.

Torque wrench. This is used for doing up screws and nuts to a specified tightness. It is a relatively expensive tool that can only be used in conjunction with a socket set, but if you intend doing any more than basic maintenance it is worth having as the small fasteners and relatively soft aluminium casting used on outboards can easily be damaged by excessive force.

Adjustable spanners. Few professional mechanics would admit to using these on an engine, because they are inevitably less rigid than proper spanners, and more likely to damage the nut or bolt as a result. Every boat, however, has at least one fastening somewhere that is an odd size. When you find out which one it is, a good adjustable will get you out of trouble. Anything less than the best is a waste of space.

Mole grips or vise grips. Like adjustable spanners, few mechanics will admit to using them, but few would be without them!

Pliers. The most useful pliers are the square-ended 'general purpose' type, about 6in long. 'Needle-nose' pliers are less versatile, but are a quite cheap and a worthwhile addition to a tool kit.

Screwdrivers. You'll inevitably need several screwdrivers, including a couple of cross-point screwdrivers and three or four flat-bladed ones, including a small 'electrician's' and a long-shafted 'heavy duty'. Handle shapes are a matter of personal choice, though the oval handles of 'carpenter's' screwdrivers may allow you to exert more force than the round handles of 'mechanic's' screwdrivers. If your heavy duty screwdriver has a square-section shaft, you will be able to apply even more force to it by fitting a spanner to the shaft when necessary.

Allen keys (or a screwdriver with a selection of hexagonal bits) are becoming more and more important.

Hammer. This is a nasty thing to threaten an engine with, but a light ball-pein 'engineer's' hammer is worth having, as is a soft-faced hammer with a weighted nylon head instead of a lump of hardened steel.

Cutting tools. You will find a few cutting tools useful, including a small **hacksaw** and some spare blades; a **craft knife** or large **scalpel**, and perhaps a small, flat-bladed **scraper** will also earn their keep.

11

Undrowning an Engine

It's all too easy to drop an outboard overboard. That fact is recognised by the manufacturers, who usually include a section dealing with 'immersion' in their manuals. Unfortunately, they rarely say more than 'take it to your nearest authorised dealer', or words to that effect – which isn't terribly useful if the disaster has struck on the Friday of a bank holiday weekend, or in a remote anchorage. Fortunately, most small outboards that are modern enough to have electronic ignition systems respond well to simple first aid treatment.

Note, however, that the process shown here does not apply to four-strokes, or to engines that have been dropped overboard while actually running. For these, or if you do not feel able to cope with this process, the best treatment is to leave the engine fully immersed – in fresh water if possible but in sea water if not – until you can get it to a professional.

Prompt action

Immediate action is essential: once an engine that has been immersed in salt water is exposed to the air, corrosion begins almost at once and if it is not running within a few hours (not a day or two!) it may never go again.

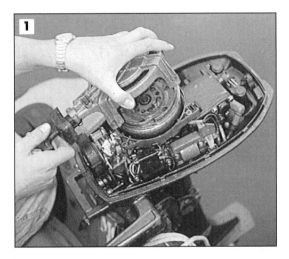

1 Remove the cowl, spark plug(s), air filter, and recoil starter mechanism.

2 Flush the ignition electrics with fresh water, directed through the holes in the flywheel and under its rim. You cannot make the engine any wetter than it is, so do not be afraid to use plenty of water to flush away the salt. If possible, use a hose pipe, otherwise use something like a washing up liquid bottle to produce a good penetrating jet.

3 Separate any obvious electrical connections, making sure that they are colour-coded and making a note of what goes where, and then flush those too. Pay particular attention to the spark plug cap.

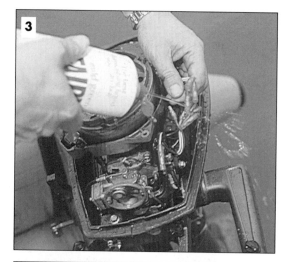

4 Lay the engine down so that the spark plug holes are uppermost, and pour water into the cylinders while slowly turning the flywheel to flush the salt water out of the cylinder, transfer port, crankcase, and carburettor.

5 Turn the engine over so that the carburettor is uppermost, and pour water down the carburettor throat, to flush it through the other way.

6 Use rags to dry the engine as best you can, and then spray the ignition system liberally with a water-displacing oil such as WD40, Duck Oil, or TS10. Spray the electrical connections, too, and reconnect all except the stop switch and kill-cord switch. (They will almost certainly have 'shorted out' and will stop the engine working if they are connected.)

7 Refit the recoil starter, mount the engine in its usual running position, and pull the

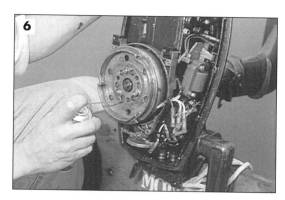

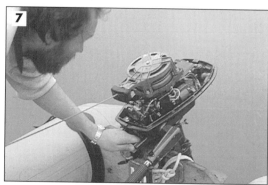

starter briskly and repeatedly until no more water sprays out of the spark plug hole(s).

8 Spray water repellent oil into the cylinder through the spark plug hole and into the crankcase through the carburettor, turning the engine with the starter as you do so.

9 Clean and dry the spark plug, and check that there is a spark by attaching the plug lead, resting or clamping the plug on a bare metal part of the engine, and then pulling the starter while looking and listening for the spark. If there is no spark, check the electrical connections, and make sure you have not reconnected the stop switch or kill switch.

10 Unscrew the drain plug from the carburettor float chamber, or improvise by removing the float chamber bowl, and then pump fuel through the system by squeezing the primer bulb if it has a remote tank or by spinning the crankshaft with the starter. Have a container ready to catch any fuel that comes out. Then close the drain plug or re-fit the float bowl.

11 Clean and dry the spark plug and re-fit it. Attach the plug lead, and re-fit the air filter. Give the engine full throttle and choke, and try to start the engine.

12 The chances are that more water will be driven out of the crankcase into the cylinder, so that after a few pulls it will become more difficult to spin the engine. If so, remove the spark plug and pull the starter cord a few more times to expel the water from the cylinder.

13 Repeat stages **11** and **12** until the engine starts. Then run it under load for at least an

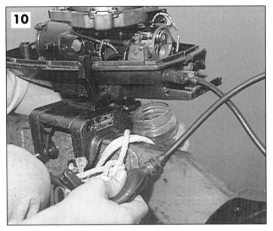

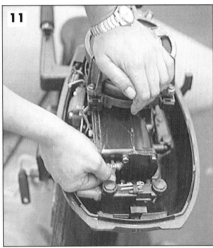

hour, if possible using a richer than usual oil:fuel mixture (up to double the usual quantity of oil) to dry the whole engine off and to coat its working parts with oil.

14 Take the engine to an outboard mechanic for a thorough strip-down and inspection.

12

Maintenance and Fault-finding

Watch any public slipway on a sunny weekend, and sooner or later you'll see someone with a troublesome outboard. It's not that outboards are inherently unreliable: quite the reverse. It's just that most of them suffer the twin perils of lack of use and lack of maintenance.

The majority of problems, however, are down to operator error (such as feeding the engine with the wrong mixture of fuel and oil), to the inadvertent operation of one of the safety interlocks incorporated in the engine (such as short-circuiting the kill switch), or to various problems with the fuel supply.

The fault-finding charts are not intended to be a comprehensive guide to every possible fault that might afflict a sophisticated engine, but they should provide a straightforward and logical way of diagnosing the most common problems.

Flooding

'Flooding' refers to the condition that arises when an engine has received fuel without burning it, so the inside of the engine is wet. Simply leaving the engine alone for ten minutes is often enough to cure minor flooding, but if you want to take more positive action, the first thing to do is to remove the spark plugs and disconnect the fuel line. Open the choke (ie push the knob in!)

and – with the kill cord disconnected so that there's no risk of a spark from the plug leads – turn the engine over repeatedly by hand or on the starter.

Check that the tilt is working and that there is no debris round the prop.

Testing for a spark

To test for a spark you should first clean away any fuel that may be in the vicinity, to reduce the risk of fire. Then, devise some method of clamping the plug to the bare metal of the engine. As a last resort, you can hold it in contact by hand, using a pair of well-insulated pliers, but beware that you are dealing with very high voltages, so a bit of damp rag will not do. Turn the engine over using the starter while watching and listening for a small but powerful blue spark across the electrodes of the plug. In bright sunlight, you may be able to hear the crack of the spark better than you can see it.

. . . Things to do

Checking spark plug condition

A Normal. Light tan to grey colour of insulator indicates correct heat range.

B Core bridging. This may be caused by either excessive carbon in the cylinder, the use of non-recommended oils or improper fuel:oil ratio.

C Wet fouling. Damp or wet, black carbon coating over entire firing end of plug. Caused by either spark plug heat range too cold, pro-longed low speed operation, low speed carburettor adjust-ment too rich or improper fuel:oil ratio.

D Gap bridging. Similar to core bridging, except the combustion particles are wedged or fused between the electrodes. The causes are the same.

E Overheating. Badly worn electrodes and premature gap wear along with a grey or white 'blistered' appearance on the insula-tor. Caused by one or more of the following:

• Spark plug range too hot

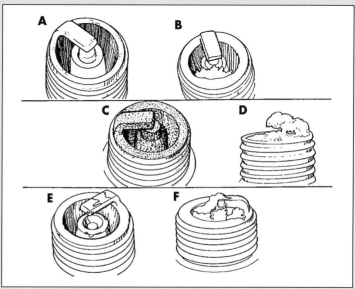

• Incorrect propeller
• Worn or defective water pump
• Restricted water intake or restriction some where in the cooling system.

F Ash deposits or lead fouling. Ash deposits are light brown to white in colour and result from use of fuel or oil additives. Lead fouling produces a yellowish brown discoloration and can be avoided by using unleaded fuels.

Drawing by courtesy of Clymer Publications, a division of Intertec Publishing

Daily maintenance

Before starting:

- Check that the engine is securely clamped to the boat.

- Check that you have an adequate supply of the right fuel or fuel:oil mixture.

- Check oil level (*four-strokes only*).

- Turn the steering from lock to lock a couple of times.

- Make sure there is no debris around the propeller.

- Do NOT, under any circumstances, start the engine without cooling water.

- Make sure the fuel tap is open and the fuel tank vent is open.

After starting

- Check that there is an adequate flow of cooling water through the tell-tale.

- Allow the engine to warm up at a fast tick-over before using it.

After use

- If possible, run the engine with fresh water cooling, using either a water tank or flush muffs.

- Make sure the fuel tap is shut, and that the fuel tank vent is shut.

- If the engine is to be left on the boat, tilt it so that the propeller and the bottom of the leg are just clear of the water.

- Grease exposed parts of steering and control cables.

- If the engine is to be removed from the boat, stand it upright for a few seconds, to allow the water to drain from the cooling system, and then carry it with the power head slightly higher than the leg, to stop the last drips from running back up the exhaust system.

- When you lay the engine down, lie it either on its back with the front of the engine facing upwards, or on the tiller side, with the gear-shift facing upwards.

Routine maintenance

About every 25–50 hours

- Remove the propeller, remove any debris and grease the shaft.
- Grease the clamp screws, control linkages, steering and tilt pivots.

- Inspect the fuel filter, and clean or replace it if necessary.

- Clean or replace spark plugs.

- Check gearbox oil level (replace every 100 hours).

- Drain and replace engine oil every 100 hours (*four-strokes only*).

- Inspect electrical wiring and connections.

- Inspect starter cord and replace if it is frayed or worn.

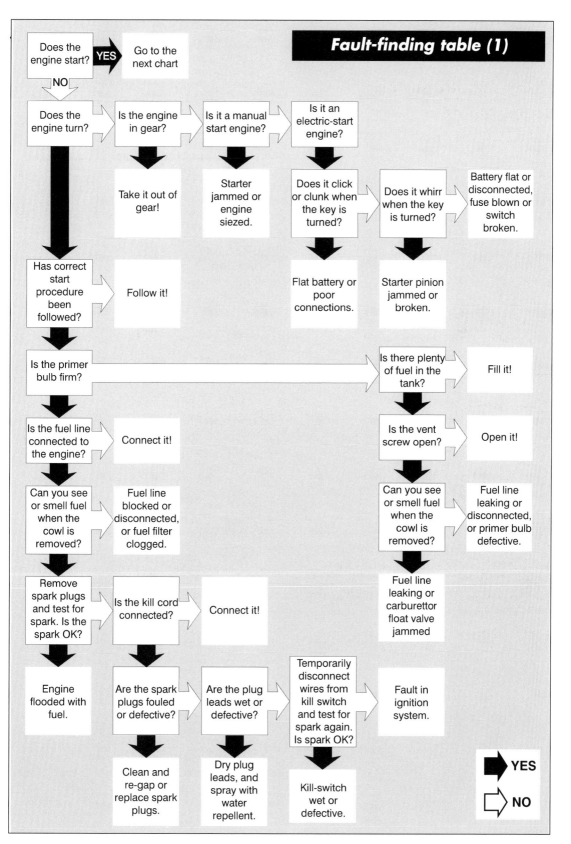

Fault-finding table (1)

Does the engine start? — YES → Go to the next chart

NO ↓

Does the engine turn? → Is the engine in gear? → Is it a manual start engine? → Is it an electric-start engine?

↓ Take it out of gear!

↓ Starter jammed or engine siezed.

Does it click or clunk when the key is turned? → Does it whirr when the key is turned? → Battery flat or disconnected, fuse blown or switch broken.

Has correct start procedure been followed? → Follow it!

Flat battery or poor connections.

Starter pinion jammed or broken.

Is the primer bulb firm? → Is there plenty of fuel in the tank? → Fill it!

Is the fuel line connected to the engine? → Connect it!

Is the vent screw open? → Open it!

Can you see or smell fuel when the cowl is removed? → Fuel line blocked or disconnected, or fuel filter clogged.

Can you see or smell fuel when the cowl is removed? → Fuel line leaking or disconnected, or primer bulb defective.

Remove spark plugs and test for spark. Is the spark OK? → Is the kill cord connected? → Connect it!

Fuel line leaking or carburettor float valve jammed

Engine flooded with fuel.

Are the spark plugs fouled or defective? → Are the plug leads wet or defective? → Temporarily disconnect wires from kill switch and test for spark again. Is spark OK? → Fault in ignition system.

Clean and re-gap or replace spark plugs.

Dry plug leads, and spray with water repellent.

Kill-switch wet or defective.

■► YES

▷ NO

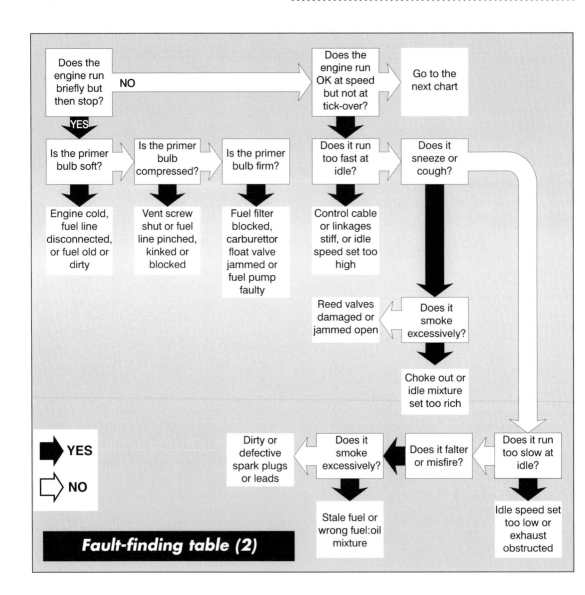

Does the engine run briefly but then stop?

NO → Does the engine run OK at speed but not at tick-over? → Go to the next chart

YES ↓

Is the primer bulb soft? → Is the primer bulb compressed? → Is the primer bulb firm?

Does it run too fast at idle? → Does it sneeze or cough?

Engine cold, fuel line disconnected, or fuel old or dirty

Vent screw shut or fuel line pinched, kinked or blocked

Fuel filter blocked, carburettor float valve jammed or fuel pump faulty

Control cable or linkages stiff, or idle speed set too high

Reed valves damaged or jammed open ← Does it smoke excessively?

Choke out or idle mixture set too rich

Dirty or defective spark plugs or leads ← Does it smoke excessively? ← Does it falter or misfire? ← Does it run too slow at idle?

Stale fuel or wrong fuel:oil mixture

Idle speed set too low or exhaust obstructed

▶ YES

▷ NO

Fault-finding table (2)

78

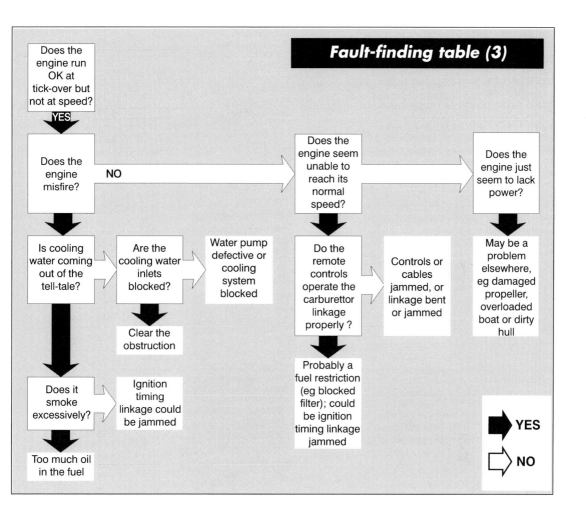

Fault-finding table (3)

Does the engine run OK at tick-over but not at speed?

YES

Does the engine misfire?

NO

Does the engine seem unable to reach its normal speed?

Does the engine just seem to lack power?

Is cooling water coming out of the tell-tale?

Are the cooling water inlets blocked?

Water pump defective or cooling system blocked

Clear the obstruction

Do the remote controls operate the carburettor linkage properly ?

Controls or cables jammed, or linkage bent or jammed

May be a problem elsewhere, eg damaged propeller, overloaded boat or dirty hull

Does it smoke excessively?

Ignition timing linkage could be jammed

Probably a fuel restriction (eg blocked filter); could be ignition timing linkage jammed

Too much oil in the fuel

▶ YES

▷ NO

79

. . . Things to do

Laying up or winterising

The main object of 'laying up' or 'winterising' is to stop the engine corroding away while it is out of sight and out of mind in a shed or locker. It's also an opportunity to do all those other routine maintenance jobs that somehow got put off during the summer!

If nothing else, though, you can do your engine a favour by storing it in a dry well-ventilated place, and not wrapping it in rags or plastic that will trap moisture.

1 Remove the engine cowling and air filter, and then run the engine up to operating temperature with cooling water supplied from flush muffs or in a flushing tank.

2 Two-strokes only: disconnect the fuel line (or shut the fuel tap) (Photo 2a) and then, before the engine stops, spray a storage sealant (such as Quicksilver Storage Seal) in through the carburettors (Photo 2b). It will produce clouds of white exhaust smoke, and the engine may splutter, but keep going until the engine stops.

. . . Things to do

3 Replace the air filter if fitted.

4 Change the engine oil (see page 39) (four-strokes only).

5 Remove the spark plugs (Photo 5a), and spray a small quantity of storage seal into each spark plug hole before replacing the plugs finger tight (Photo 5b).

6 Clean off old grease using a proprietary spray-on degreaser such as Gunk or Jizer, and hose down the engine to wash off the degreaser and any salt deposits.

7 Spray the whole power head lightly with a water-repellent oil such as WD40, TS10 or Duck Oil.

8 Re-grease control linkages.

9 Grease all grease points (see owner's manual) some points will require a grease gun to force grease into the nipple under pressure.

... Things to do

10 Change the gearbox oil. Photo 10a shows the vent plug being unscrewed. In Photo 10b, oil is being squirted into the drain plug.

11 Touch up the paintwork.

12 Replace any anti-corrosion anodes that have been eaten away to less than about 50% of their original size: there is often one fitted as a fin behind the propeller, or one or two fitted to the lower part of the leg.

Metal fuel tanks are best stored full, to reduce the risk of rust forming inside, but don't be tempted, next season, to use fuel that has been stored for several months: get rid of it and start the season with fresh fuel and clean, new spark plugs.

Acknowledgements

Sincere thanks to all those involved in the production of this book, including:

Bill Anderson and the Training Division of the RYA

Peter Dredge and the Motor Cruising Division of the RYA

Motor Boat & Yachting for the illustration on page 1

Clymer Publications, for permission to reproduce diagrams from their excellent workshop manuals on pages 16, 50, and 74

Philip Pond, for the photo on page 67
Richard Langdon of Ocean Images for the photo sequence on pages 70, 71 and 72.

Special thanks are due to Eddie Mays of Hamble for all the other photographs and to Lee Fairweather of Fairweather Marine in Fareham for wielding the spanners during Eddie's photo sessions.

All other illustrations are by the Author.

Index